Platinum-Blazing the Appalachian Trail

How to Thru-Hike in 5 3-Star Luxury

Platinum-Blazing the Appalachian Trail: How to Thru-hike in ~~5~~-3-Star Luxury

Published by Campbell & Parker Books

Photographic image of Appalachian Trail map on back cover (and in the book's interior) was provided courtesy of the Appalachian Trail Conservancy. Front cover image was work for hire. The photographic image of the authors on the back cover is provided courtesy of Michael Neiman. The other photographic images in the book's interior are provided courtesy of Bruce Matson.

ISBN: 978-0-578-47116-7

Inquiries concerning future editions, please contact The Platinum-Blaze Institute at admin@platinum-blazing.com.

Platinum-Blazing
the Appalachian Trail

How to Thru-Hike in 5 3-Star Luxury

Bruce "RTK" Matson

and

Michael "Sharkbait" Neiman

Campbell & Parker

Contents

A WELCOME FROM THE AUTHORS

Welcome to our little project on Platinum-Blazing. Every spring, thousands of individuals head for Springer Mountain in Georgia, throw on a 30-pound backpack and start walking North hoping to finish at Mt. Katahdin in Maine before Baxter State Park closes the summit trail in October. In 2018 we were part of the 5,000 or so individuals who attempted what is known as a "thru-hike" – an attempt to walk all 2,200 miles of the Appalachian Trail in a 12-month period.

Some hike southbound from Maine, others start at various spots and "flip-flop," from top to bottom to end back where they started. However, like us, nearly 90 percent of attempted thru-hikers travel northbound. Historically, only one out of four who start the hike will finish, and those who do are forever changed for it. It is a difficult endeavor to carry everything you need on your back, sleeping outdoors, surviving the elements, and dealing with the everyday trials of walking nonstop ... all without the everyday comforts of home you have grown accustomed to!

We both thru-hiked northbound (or NOBO) beginning in early 2018, a hiking season now known for its brutal winter in the south, record mid-Atlantic rainfall in the spring, and unusual New England summer heat. We both enjoyed getting off-trail to indulge in a few of the special opportunities available between Georgia to Maine – great ice cream, fine dining, premium lodging, etc. Recognizing that no hiker is going to be able to take advantage of every opportunity, we thought a guide to these special experiences and opportunities could help future thru-hikers make better decisions on how to add a bit of upscale comfort to their hike. We hope you will use this guide both planning your adventure as well as for reference during the trip. It is intended to not to replace, but to supplement your use of a guidebook (*Thru-Hiker Companion*, AWOL's *AT Guide*) or mobile app (Guthook) for every day hike support.

The gathering, collating and presentation of opinions about what is premium, or "platinum" is far from scientific or objective. We recognize that selecting the "best of" is always somewhat subjective – everyone has opinions, and not everyone will share ours. However, if you agree with our line of thinking, we believe you can look forward to and enjoy our selections. We know there will be places you feel passionately should be on one of our lists, and others that should be removed. As this guide will change year to year, we encourage you to contact us (admin@platinum-blazing.com) with your reviews, nominations, discoveries and more.

This guide is an effort for us to give back to the community that gave so much to us. In hopes that the Appalachian Trail and all of its wonderful supporters continue to be available to those who come after us, a portion of the proceeds from every book sold will be donated directly to the Appalachian Trail Conservancy.

Lastly, our apologies to AT southbound hikers but since starting a thru-hike from Springer Mountain still is the overwhelming choice by thru-hikers . . . our lists are geographically ordered as such. When making reference to a mile # as a way to help locate a restaurant, hostel, etc. we use the marker with reference to miles from the southern terminus at Springer Mountain.

- Sharkbait & RTK

WHAT IS "PLATINUM-BLAZING?"

When navigating your way through the Appalachian Mountains, every hiker needs a compass to guide them on their journey. In today's information age this is more than just a needle pointing to magnetic north. There are countless books, mobile apps, films, YouTube channels, and daily blog sites to help hikers follow their path through the woods. However, it is the original and simplest of these systems that still works best ... blazes. Thru-hikers on the Appalachian Trail find their way along the trail by following white blazes, a 2x6-inch vertical, white stripe painted on trees and rocks that mark the path. These hikers are **"White-blazing."** Neither Sharkbait nor RTK kept track, but one person did recently and claims there are over 165,000 white blazes on rocks, trees, posts and elsewhere on the AT from Georgia to Maine.

White blazes, however, are not the only trail guidance system. In addition to white, there are other painted blazes used to guide hikers forward. The most commonly known alteration to the norm is **"Blue-blazing,"** which is common and necessary during a thru-hike. Blue blazes typically signal and mark a trail that is ancillary to the white-blazed trail, including trails to shelters, water sources, and points of interest. (For more, please see our guide to the best blue-blaze points of interest in Chapter 9).

Blue blazes are also used from time to time on the Appalachian Trail to signal and mark "extreme weather" trails, where it may be unreasonably hazardous to take the primary route in wet or icy conditions (such as at the Firescald Ridge in Tennessee or around many of the hill climbs north of Prospect Rock in New York). While hiking along the AT, one might also see red blazes marking closed areas, purple blazes marking off-limit (private) areas, and other rainbow-colored blazes marking known tertiary trails. These all have a purpose in helping a thru-hiker to know which direction to continue along, and which crisscrossing paths to avoid.

Over the years, other more creative expressions of "blazing" have found their way into common backpacker vernacular as well, some of which are just as common as the physical blazes above to AT thru-hikers. For example, someone who is **"Yellow-blazing"** travels portions of the AT by car, along streets and roads often marked with familiar yellow divider lanes, instead of hiking with the white blazes. Yellow-blazing can also be common on foot, where someone decides to road or street walk portions of Trail that are parallel or intersect sections of the Trail. Yellow-blazing is fairly simple and can give thru-hikers an easier shortcut to the trail. The Blue Ridge Parkway and Skyline Drive in Virginia are especially common areas for yellow-blazing.

As the popularity of thru-hiking has grown, hikers have had fun with this concept of alternative blazing over the years. Some of the more common extensions that can be heard on the trail these days include:

- **Web-blazing** or **silk-blazing** refers to hiking through spider webs, which are typically (and uncomfortably) caught by your face. This is, of course, most common when you are the first on the trail in the morning.

- **Pink-blazing** refers to the highly discouraged behavior of some hikers (most typically young males) to hike after (follow and pursue) other, fellow hikers on the trail (most typically young women).

- **Green-blazing** refers to the practice of smoking marijuana regularly on the trail (or following those who can provide it).

- **Aqua-blazing** is another common way to shortcut walking the white blazes, as it suggests using waterways along the trail to move forward on a thru-hike. Aqua-blazing is really only done along Shenandoah National Park by floating north on the Shenandoah River from Waynesboro to Harper's Ferry. There really is no other place on the AT to travel any of its length for any appreciable distance by water.

- **Retro-blazing** refers to hiking portions of the historical AT (i.e., a former route or path that has been removed or rerouted. Like aqua-blazing, the reference to retro-blazing is typically not for nostalgia, but to justify a shortcut or easier way to move along the Trail on a hike. A common example is the mile road walk north out of Unionville, NY (previously the AT followed this road, but has since been rerouted through the woods outside of town). Appalachian Trail historians will note that much of the "original" trail was mapped along state roads, so retro-blazing is often also akin to yellow-blazing.

There are many other physical (and metaphysical) types of blazing you may hear about during the planning and execution of a thru-hike, some common and some seemingly being made up every year by excited young hikers. (We highlight "deli-blazing" in the Appendix; and in our discussion of "Slackpacking" below in Chapter 3, we introduce "lift-blazing" – a term we had not heard before on the AT or elsewhere.) All of these blaze types are meant to be directional guideposts, motivational or navigational tools to help you find your way through America's Appalachian Trail

Because of the diversity of people pursuing thru-hiker status each year, this book (and its authors) aims to identify another option for blazing your way between Georgia and Maine – **"Platinum-Blazing,"** which is the practice of enjoying the Appalachian Trail's life of luxury. Platinum-Blazing, then, is the practice of enjoying the finer or premium off-trail opportunities for meals, accommodations and related activities. Some of these are further off-trail than most hikers experience, but all can be visited easily as part of your hike if desired, and some are focused on activities other than walking each day (blasphemy to a "purist" thru-hiker with an agenda to walk only and all steps of the white-blazed trail). An example would be choosing to stay at a nice bed & breakfast in town rather than to stay in a bunk room at the hostel just feet off the trail. For example, in Roan Mountain, TN a hiker can stay at Roan Mountain B&B or grab a bunk at Station 19. Or, the same thru-hiker in that town can choose either option at the same place: Mountain Harbour B&B. (And, by the way, each of these properties makes one or more of our lists below!)

To emphasize the concept (as it is the primary focus of this guide), here are a few examples of the luxury activities that we consider indicative of Platinum-Blazing (all of these are actual experiences we learned about or enjoyed personally during our 2018 thru-hikes):

- Reserving a private cabin at the Misty Mountain Inn at Neel Gap, instead of staying in the Mountain Crossings bunkhouse.
- Attending a theatrical play onsite while enjoying the exceptional accommodations at Allenberry Resort in Boiling Springs, PA.
- Enjoying an elegant dinner and private room at the Fife 'n Drum Inn of Kent, CT
- Ordering an a la carte steak dinner when the restaurant has an AYCE buffet, like at Daniel's Restaurant in Hiawassee, GA.
- Indulging in a natural "hot springs" whirlpool appointment in Hot Springs, NC.
- Getting a full body massage at the Woods Hole Hostel.
- Slackpacking from Hot Springs, NC to Damascus, VA while enjoying private accommodations at Cantarroso Farm each night.
- Renting out the Airstream private trailer at the Hikers Inn in Damascus, VA
- Scheduling an Uber to pick you up at the Dover Oak and take you to the Station Inn at Pawling, NY
- Taking a guided, fly-fishing excursion during a day off the Trail in North Woodstock, NH
- Enjoying a whitewater rafting trip down the Kennebec River outside Caratunk, ME

One of the less obvious, but most available ways to Platinum-Blaze is to take full advantage of the Appalachian Mountain Club (AMC) huts found throughout the White Mountains in New Hampshire. Staying at these AMC huts (which typically costs over $100 a night) provides a special or even premium "shelter" experience because overnight guests not only get a bunk (with pillows and blankets) in a building with four walls and a roof (and toilets and running water), but they are treated to what are essentially all-you-can-eat, family-style dinners and breakfasts.

Because of the more limited tenting opportunities along this part of the Trail, planning your overnight stops can be a challenge. Thru-hikers often try to do "work-for-stay" (WFS) at the AMC huts, where they receive dinner (and often breakfast the next morning) as well as permission to sleep on the dining room floor in exchange for an hour or two of work (typically washing dishes, sweeping, and other tasks). When RTK inquired about how he might work his way through the White Mountains a former thru-hiker explained how he hiked this rugged part of the Trail by staying *each night* in one of these mountain huts.

As it turns out, with a little bit of planning, thru-hikers can experience the full-service offerings at any or *all* of these huts – something we call "hut-blazing," an impressive form or subset of Platinum-Blazing. In fact, Sharkbait used this very same strategy for his time in the White Mountains, booking reservations or leveraging WFS all the way to Gorham, NH. (RTK did similar choosing WFS at Lake of the Clouds and paying for nights at Zealand Falls and Carter Notch.)

Advance reservations and careful planning are often required to stay at the AMC huts. Although difficult, coordinating your hiking schedule to meet reservation dates is possible with a bit of flexibility. Later in this book, we'll show you how to take advantage of some well-placed days off before and after the White Mountains, to take in the full AMC Hut experience.

WHY THIS GUIDE?

During one's hike, every thru-hiker needs to come off the Trail; if nothing else, to at least resupply their rations of food for the next few days. Most thru-hikers also come off the Trail occasionally to do laundry, shower, rest tired feet, pick-up miscellaneous supplies, recharge batteries, or attend to other personal needs. In addition to those matters, most thru-hikers look to get off the Trail just to feel normal again … have a real meal, not consisting of instant ramen or potatoes, and to sleep in an actual bed. There is no shortage of ways to recharge one's mental batteries with a night in town, and every hiker needs it from time to time as they pass through and by Trail Towns.

This guide assumes that the time a hiker takes off the trail involves experiences that will ultimately make his or her thru-hike more rewarding. How frequently one might enjoy town visits for meals or lodging will inevitably depend, in no small degree, on the size of the particular thru-hiker's budget as well as the time allotted for the trip. Understandably, many hikers, particularly those in the common demographic of twentysomethings and recent college graduates, have limited budgets. Although Platinum-Blazing comes with different financial expectations, any of the experiences identified here can still be enjoyed by every hiker … the quantity and consistency may simply differ for those who choose to indulge more often.

One of our fellow 2018 thru-hikers that inspired us to write this guide was Sally Forth, who (with pride) admits having hut-blazed the entire White Mountains, slackpacked wherever possible, rarely slept on the ground, and even found a way to purchase a pedicure no less than once a week. While it is certainly possible, this book does not expect many hikers will take advantage of every special opportunity identified here. However, this guide will attempt to highlight places where a special, "platinum" experience is available as an option. Also, some of the best experiences – like communal meals, spontaneous activities, food challenges, etc. – are located at hostels that themselves might not be considered platinum, however, since the activity or experience itself is, they are well worth noting.

This book, then, is an effort to collect the very best of the experiences available to thru-hikers, and to give them the information to help choose them appropriately. It was inspired in part by RTK's trek on the Camino de Santiago. During that walk he missed some of the iconic places and unique experiences mostly because he was not alerted to them until it was too late – better planning would have made those experiences not just more likely, but a priority. We hope this guide helps thru-hikers make the most of their time off the Trail and whenever possible slow down long enough to "smell the roses" and enjoy the finer things along the Trail.

Similarly, Sharkbait spent years and years preparing for his AT hike, reading countless biographies and journals of others on the trail, and taking notes on the special and lavish experiences he read about and wanted to make sure to hit. A book like this would have helped summarize the best trail stops to include in one place, saving countless (wasted) hours comparing one hiker's reason for stay somewhere against another's reason to miss it.

In the end, no one person's experience can ever encompass every trail stop, so we wrote this guide to identify list the best experiences a luxury hiker should try to include. In reading this guide, you will see all the great recommendations in one place and be able to identify which platinum experiences are best for you as you take on your own thru-hike.

Other guidebooks, like those provided by AWOL and the ATC, have useful waypoint and logistical information, but no qualitative evaluation of hostels, restaurants or other experiences – and little attention to the more exceptional experiences available. While thru-hiking the Trail in 2018, the authors stayed at many different hostels, hotels, and town. Some were known and sought out because of the anticipated unique experience (like Woods Hole Hostel), but others were unknown and unheard of ... and turned out to be great experiences (like Quarter Way Inn and Rock 'n Sole). In talking with other hikers, we know there are even more that we both missed, such as Creekside Paradise B&B (Fontana Dam, TN) and Caffé Rel (Franklin, NC). If we had this guide, we might have enjoyed those stops (or at least, considered them properly) and avoided using limited, valuable off-trail time and resources on more marginal choices. We hope that a book like this can help avoid that same problem for future thru-hike adventurers.

While this guide is really about the very best, premier or platinum places and experiences, it also calls out honorable mentions and up & comers where applicable. These places and experiences might not today be considered platinum today - but they should not be ignored, as they may work their way up to the platinum ranks in the future.

Deer Head Inn (Delaware Water Gap, PA)

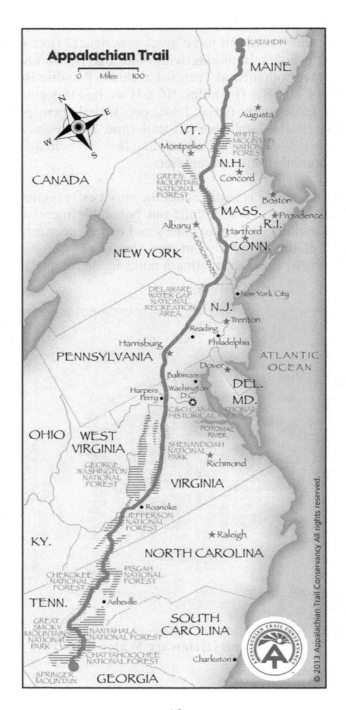

Appalachian Trail

0   Miles   100

18

Chapter 1

"OFF TRAIL" TOWN VISITS

When you encounter someone on the AT, they can typically be categorized as a day hiker, section hiker, or thru-hiker. As the name suggests, a day hiker is out on the Trail just for the day, typically carrying just a "day pack" containing water, snacks or lunch and an extra clothing layer or rain gear. A section hiker is focused on hiking the entire Appalachian Trail during their lifetime, a "section" at a time. A "thru-hiker" then is one who attempts to hike the entire Appalachian Trail during a single 12-month period.

Not surprisingly, as a project of two individuals who just completed hiking the entire way from Georgia to Maine by way of the AT, this guide was written initially with the "thru-hiker" in mind. A thru-hiker expects to "touch" every white blaze and suffer through vagaries of weather, the monotony of trail food, the absence of loved ones, and the often-brutal conditions of the footpath. It's a 2,200-mile journey over diverse terrain with cumulative climbs and descents of over 464,000 feet – reputed to be equivalent to climbing up and down Mt. Everest sixteen times. A thru-hike is difficult. So, obviously, thru-hikers revel in opportunities to stop into towns for a shower, resupply, laundry and perhaps to splurge on lodging or meal, or both!

While a few suggest that they are engaged in a "pure" hike, every thru-hiker comes off the Trail and goes into town during their months traversing the woods. Earl Shaffer, the first person to complete a thru-hike of the AT, came off the trail occasionally ... and every thru-hiker since (except some extreme examples of "supported" hikes) has had to do the same. At a minimum, town visits are *necessary* to resupply rations – obviously no one can carry all the provisions needed for a four to seven-month sojourn. This is often done by stopping at a grocery store to acquire food for the next 3-5 days. Walmart is a hiker favorite, due to its big selection and small prices, but frequently a gas station convenience store has to make do. A Platinum-Blazer might go searching for Whole Foods or a New York deli to make meals on the trail a bit more lavish as well.

Thru-hikers will get to a nearby town many different ways. One can always walk of course, but other common options are hitchhiking, mass transit, shuttle drivers, or ride-shares (e.g. Uber). For example:

• **Walking.** This one is obvious, and what thru-hikers do best. But most hikers prefer not to add additional steps to the 2,200 miles they've already committed to. That said, it's not unusual for thru-hikers to walk 2 or 3 miles to get into a town when needed. Let's just say, such a diversion by foot is rarely part of Platinum-Blazing. And, it's worth mentioning that the AT thru-hiker actually walks through a number of towns like Hot Springs, NC, Damascus, VA, and Dalton, MA.

• **Hitchhiking.** Another common option though can be difficult to succeed with in some places (and illegal in others). Typically, many who undertake a 2-mile walk from the trail into town, start off by hoping to hitch a ride instead. Although an improvement from walking, hitchhiking rarely accompanies a platinum experience (unless no better options are available).

• **Mass Transit.** There are opportunities to use public transportation (such as Harpers Ferry, WV, and a few towns around New York, such as Pawling, NY) and some localities have regional bus or trolley services (such as Marion, VA). But again, there's nothing "platinum" about mass transit.

• **Shuttles.** In planning a town visit, especially for a Platinum-Blazer, a thru-hiker may want first to select his or her overnight option. It is very common for a hostel, B&B or motel to offer a free or modestly priced pick-up and drop-off shuttle service. In addition to those provided as lodging amenities, many additional shuttle services exist from independent entrepreneurs up and down the trail to various sites for nominal fees.

- **Taxis/Rideshare/Shuttle**. Often, but not everywhere, thru-hikers can call a car service for a ride. In more rural areas, there are typically some local taxis and/or independent shuttle drivers, but in more populated areas (like Fort Montgomery or Pawling, NY), one can leverage Uber and Lyft quite easily.

- **Trail Angels.** Many trail towns have amazing individuals who simply love the AT and its hikers and will offer free rides from time to time. Finding these individuals may be more difficult; however, some are listed in the popular published guides, some are mentioned in the comment sections of Guthook waypoints, some may be on hiker kiosks at trailheads, and some more organized trail towns like Waynesboro and Hanover actually produce a list. We think using Trail Angels for such rides may be part of a platinum experience because of the knowledgeable, interesting, and generous people you can meet (such as Jim Sparks, who offers rides for any donation amount near Marion, VA).

Town visits are also crucial for doing chores, such as laundry, showering, and repairing or replacing gear. While in town for resupply or these other activities, thru-hikers often look to enjoy the "real" food so lacking on the Trail – fresh fruits and vegetables, burgers and pizza, grilled steak, ethnic cuisine, or generally anything to curb one's cravings and hiker hunger. It's nearly impossible to catalog and rate every meal option off-trail, but we will highlight the more special restaurants and meal options not to be missed; for example, breakfast at Quarter Way Inn (Atkins, VA), dinner at Caffé Rel (Franklin, NC), or Mulligan's famous Applewood smoked wings (Manchester Center, VT). Platinum-Blazers are not focused primarily on quantity, so we do not highlight the popular AYCE options in town, which the standard guides do reasonably well anyway.

When appropriate we may comment on the value proposition, but this guide does not focus on nor provide detailed cost breakdowns. By definition, a hiker engaged in Platinum-Blazing is willing to pay more than is otherwise typical. Thus, unless we thought the charge was exorbitant, we do not routinely comment on the individual cost of a meal or services. Instead, we direct you to places we consider excellent, and worthy of the Platinum label, and trust you will make the final decision about the cost and value that is right for you. For us, Platinum-Blazing enhances the thru-hike experience rather than detracting from or limiting the challenge or sense of accomplishment.

Sharkbait (rain kilt and all)

Chapter 2

YOUR PERSONAL CONCIERGE

The purest form of Platinum-Blazing includes the thru-hiker's regular use of an assistant or travel planner to make calls and arrangements for shuttles, private accommodations, and related needs. We like to call this special type of trail angel a "personal concierge."

Ideally, your personal concierge will be a co-worker, family member, or good friend that is interested (sincerely) in your hike. While a spouse is a logical candidate at first, we urge you to consider thoroughly the wisdom of making calls regularly to your husband/wife to have them book dinner reservations and spa treatments when they are trying to keep things together at home while you enjoy a 5- or 6-month vacation on the Appalachian Trail. That's not to say that there aren't many spouses/partners who would fill that role happily ... in fact, Sharkbait met a platinum concierge named Sherpa in the Smokey Mountains, who supported his thru-hiking girlfriend by following along in a van and taking her to motels each night. That said, we suggest you but think long and hard about asking a significant other to be your personal concierge. During our hike, we each had the benefit of personal concierge from time to time. For RTK, this was a law firm paralegal, co-worker and friend back home in Richmond. For Sharkbait, it was a sister that lived in the Washington DC metro area.

At times having a personal concierge might seem to be more luxury than necessity, but it is a true sign of Platinum-Blazing ... and one you'll be glad you have. While cell coverage on the AT is extensive and improving every day, thru-hikers still have many areas and particular spots where no access to cellular reception exists. Yes, even if you use Verizon. Furthermore, bad weather and/or trail conditions often make it difficult and dangerous to hike, and even harder to make off-trail arrangements – perhaps when needed most. You won't realize how important your personal concierge is, until you are trying to Google nearby motels for a vacancy, while hiking in a thunderstorm of pouring rain. It can be incredibly useful to have someone dialing around for a reservation or a driver while you attend to the hike. Otherwise, you may be searching for good reception or awaiting a return call when it is too cold to stand still, and too wet for a touchscreen to respond to soaked fingers effectively.

During our hike, both of us were caught in a winter snowstorm that required platinum upgrades. For RTK, this was outside Hot Springs, NC, where snow was quickly accumulating and drifting around him:

> *The temperature was below freezing, and the wind was blowing. Cell coverage was spotty. I was most concerned near the summit of Bluff Mountain because the drifts started to obliterate the footprints of hikers ahead of me, making the trail hard to follow. With the wind blowing, snow was also sticking to the trees, making white blazes harder to pick out. As snow began to drift above my knees, I knew I could likely not make the intended shelter ... and if I did, it would probably be full of hikers I knew were in front of me. I was alone.*

> *With snow accumulating up to 10 inches (drifting up to three feet) and still falling, I wondered what I should do and weighed what I realistically could do. I would have to find a tenting spot soon and set up in a foot of snow. I pulled out my phone to use the Guthook App to try to see if there was a camping site nearby. I noticed I had cell coverage near the top of Bluff Mountain. I texted Stacy, but I needed to keep hiking in light of the temperature and precipitation. Stacy found a shuttle driver who could meet me at a gravel road trailhead. And she found a room in Hot Springs, which was heavily booked due to the weather. I averted a potentially life-threatening situation.*

RTK's episode on Bluff Mountain was nearly an emergency, but his personal concierge helped save him from a disaster on the Trail. In addition, on many other occasions, it was a luxury to have someone assisting with logistics while he enjoyed his hiking experience.

It is also very important to equip your personal concierge with the right tools to aid you. Whether you are using AWOL's AT Guide, the ATC's Thru-hiker's Companion, Guthook App, or other resource ... be sure to equip your personal concierge with their own copy, as well as a copy of this guide. Furthermore, you should provide an overview and basic understanding of your hike, including issues like resupply and planned town visits – your personal concierge can certainly be more helpful if they better understand the conditions and struggles of a thru-hike. Lastly, to be most effective, your personal concierge will ideally need specific personal information to best support your travels, including the following:

- Credit card information (including billing address and CSV codes)

- Usernames and passwords to certain websites that facilitate the use of hotel and other travel websites (e.g. Orbitz or Travelocity).

- Shared location alerts via a GPS or cellular device (e.g. SPOT, InReach, or Apple's "Find Friends" app).

- A list of planned hostel and city stops with addresses, for delivery/forwarding of packages.

- Emergency contact information (for emergencies).

- Any other personal details so they can act on your behalf

Both of us purchased an AWOL Guide for our personal concierges, as it was the guidebook we used for our daily planning on the trail as well. This allowed them to understand better where we were, and what was available to help. Both the AWOL guide and Thru-hiker's companion (as well as Guthook App) have much of the contact information required to arrange a shuttle, make a hotel reservation, etc. Though as mentioned before, there are a considerable number of shuttle drivers that are not listed in the traditional guides. One last recommendation is to invite them to any social media pages or online forums you frequent where they can post questions and requests ... for example, the official Appalachian Trail group on Facebook is extremely quick and helpful to respond to trail pickup requests.

One additional role a personal concierge might play for you, is that of assisting blog or vlog publication. Many thru-hikers like to use written or video publications to share their story regularly with friends and family back home. If they are interested (and skilled appropriately), this is a great way for your personal concierge to be a larger part in your hike experience, while helping you to tell your story better. Since your personal concierge will be familiar with to the intricacies of the Trail, they will be well equipped to edit your publications on your behalf. Some ways to take advantage of this opportunity are:

- Email your journal entries, so they can edit and publish it to a blog site like WordPress.

- Share a photo album from your phone, so they can create and publish videos to a vlog site like YouTube.

- Share your social media accounts, so they can extend your reach by sharing a post from one place to another like Facebook, Instagram or Twitter.

Although a personal concierge is not always needed to publish regular journal, blog or vlog updates, it can be a valuable addition to the experience. For example, you are limited with what functionality exists on a mobile device, so having someone who can edit your content with supplemental content or functionality from a real computer can be a nice addition.

Chapter 3

SLACKPACKING

When a thru-hiker can cover some of his or her daily miles without their full backpack, it is commonly referred to as "slackpacking." Many purists on the Trail may think it blasphemy to move forward without a full backpack, but many others will take every opportunity to do so. For this reason, you may think it highly unlikely to find a purist who has much interest in Platinum-Blazing at all. But, once they have 500 or so miles under their boots, that tune is commonly. changed. A lot of stubborn purists may look lovingly at a slackpack opportunity by the time they reach Virginia.

Although there does not appear to be a generally accepted "rule" for slackpacking on a thru-hike, everyone agrees on the general idea slackpacking represents. For this book, we define slackpacking as a day's worth of thru-hiking unencumbered by a full backpack. Whether your base weight begins at 15 pounds or 50, slackpacking is the practice of alleviating most of one's belongings from burden. This is possible because of the other component of slackpacking ... a planned end-point at a place of lodging, or to a vehicle that will take you to one.

With a pre-determined bed for the night (most often where you spent the previous night), slackpacking allows you to leave your tent, sleeping bag, extra food, etc. at your destination and hike back to them with just the bare essentials. Slackpacking typically requires coordination with a shuttle ride (often provided by a hostel) and allows one to pick up where they left off in the morning. Although there are many iterations of slackpacking or "assisted hiking" that can be done to support one's thru-hike, the idea remains the same anywhere along the trail: covering some portion of miles for a day using only a stripped-down version of your backpack, a loaner daypack, or no pack at all during the day's hike.

While it is likely to be obvious, the use - especially the frequent and/or extended use of slackpacking is a useful tool in the Platinum-Blazer's toolbox. As one combines the services of a personal concierge with slackpacking opportunities, the almost luxurious or "platinum" nature of the activity becomes apparent. With a simple call or text, you can have a driver waiting for you and a day's hike unencumbered by unnecessary weight. Looking for ways to combine slackpacking with other platinum experiences is where Platinum-Blazing becomes as much an *art* as an opportunity. RTK was able to couple a slackpack through the Roan Highlands with a stay at the exceptional Roan Mountain B&B, all arranged by his personal concierge.

Besides the relief that comes with the usual 30-40 pounds being reduced to 5-10, slackpacking can also provide the added benefit of putting more miles behind you in less time. For Sharkbait, slackpacking on the Appalachian Trail provided a welcomed, and much needed change of pace:

> *After four straight days of rain hiking along the Blue Ridge Parkway in Virginia, my morale was low and attitude getting steadily saltier as the week progressed. With more rain expected over the weekend, I decided to take up an offer from family to get an assisted slackpack the next day for a change of pace. The elevation looked calm, and the promise of a warm bed did a good job of motivating my feet in the wet. My sister picked me up from a road crossing and we spent that night at a hotel in Lexington, VA.*

> *The next day, I set out a water bottle, water filter, lunch and other small essentials in my nephew's daypack. The whole pack weighed less than 5 pounds, and the only other thing I carried were my trusty hiking poles. With no heavy gear limitations, I effortlessly jogged up and down the trail at a record pace, covering 25 miles in just over 6 hours.*

28

Finishing my daily quota early, I was picked up in the early afternoon and spent the evening celebrating with a hot dinner and warm bed back in Lexington. Without the typical strain on my back and pain on my feet, the weather was more tolerable and the day's hike much more manageable. The hot tub awaiting me at the hotel didn't hurt either . . .

Although there are rare situations like Sharkbait's above, a thru-hiker's slackpack more often involves a hostel that will shuttle you forward on the Trail. With a two-night stay, many hostels will provide a complimentary shuttle ride further up the Trail in the morning from which you hike back to the hostel. Most often, this is the opposite direction from your usual route (e.g., a northbound hiker will get dropped off further north on the Trail, then hike southbound back to the hostel at their own pace).

A slackpack, though, is not necessarily just a pleasant way to more easily walk in the woods. A couple of the AT's most popular slackpacks are over the Wildcats between Pinkham Notch and Gorham (promoted by Rattle River Lodge & Hostel) and between Kinsman Notch and Franconia Notch (provided daily by The Notch Hostel) . . .both of which are through portions of the grueling White Mountains. Even without a pack, these slackpacks present a rugged and strenuous day. Here's how RTK processed it all:

In my pre-trip planning, I had planned to take advantage of both the Kinsman Slackpack and the Wildcats Slackpack. However, I found the Whites to be even more difficult than originally imagined. In talks with passing southbounders, most confirmed just how brutal South Kinsman and the Wildcats were going to be. Although I had done a few 20+ mile slackpack days already, I decided both the 19 through the Kinsmans and 20 through the Wildcats (which included one of the five steepest sections anywhere on the AT) were going to be too difficult, even with little on my back.

Slackpacking can come into play for strategic elevation purposes as well. Although not immediately intuitive to inexperienced hikers, thru-hikers typically would *prefer* to climb a steep slope than to descend it. For this reason, you'll often see slackpacking options arranged to avoid steep declines from time to time. In fact, one of the most common slackpack scenarios is to hike southbound over Mt. Moosilauke just before the White Mountains. northbound thru-hikers will stay at the Hiker's Welcome Hostel in Glencliff, NH, take a shuttle to Kinsman Notch, and hike back southward back to the hostel. In doing so, hikers can climb *up* the treacherously steep and slippery 1.5-mile north side of Moosilauke, as opposed to descending down through those dangerous conditions. While far from obvious or intuitive, hikers quickly learn that the stress-imposed in descending, including the forward push promoted by gravity, makes hiking downhill more difficult, dangerous and stressful throughout the day.

One additional thing to note for slackpacking, . . . another shuttle ride is needed the following morning to return you back to the location from where you began your southbound slackpack the prior day. It is for this unsurprisingly reason that many hostels offer free or discounted shuttles for slackpacking to and from their location.

Although this scenario is the most common example, a wide variety of other arrangements are of course possible, depending on your hiking style. Reverse slackpacking may not be ideal for thru-hiker purists who believe you should only hike the trail in one direction sequentially. Slackpacking is still possible with this mindset, though somewhat more difficult as it involves hiking north from the hostel or motel, and then being picked up again after a specified amount of mileage at a specified place at a specified time. The disadvantage to this approach is predicting when you will arrive at the pickup point at the end of the slackpack day. As this is harder on a hostel providing shuttle service to many hikers, it is sometimes less likely to be an available option. However, one advantage to this option is that it allows one to control your departure time – a hiker can leave the hostel or motel whenever they like. This is especially ideal to very early risers that do not wish to waste a morning waiting for the arranged shuttle drop-off.

RTK slackpacked often during his thru-hike, taking advantage of the opportunity to hike lighter over more miles. One example over a two-day span allowed him to slackpack southbound and northbound consecutively:

While staying at Boots Off hostel, forty-three miles from Damascus, I caught a ride with two fellow hikers whose mother was in the area. We were driven twenty-one miles north and hiked back to the hostel to stay another night. Then, the following day, I learned that a group of young hikers were going to do a forty-three-mile marathon - slackpacking all the way from Boots Off to Damascus, which required paying a shuttle to drive their gear up to Damascus. My cabin mate and I dumped most of our gear into trash bags and gave them to the shuttle driver who (after dropping us back off where I started the previous day), took our gear and the marathoners' belongings to Damascus. When I arrived at the Old Mill hotel in Damascus (a platinum choice), the trash bags full of our gear were waiting for us.

There are countless options to slackpack along the Trail, and many of our fellow hikers found numerous opportunities to do so. RTK's friend Scars reported that he slackpacked most of the Whites and Southern Maine. In Erwin, Tennessee Mike and Peggy run the Cantarroso Farm, where Mike also operates shuttles. He reported that once he slackpacked a couple of 60-something guys all the way from Erwin to Damascus, Virginia. RTK and Sharkbait spoke with many other shuttle drivers who had similar stories of slackpacking thru-hikers for multiple days and over 100 trail miles over those days. And at least one couple is known to have slackpacked the entire Appalachian Trail!

For most, thinking about slackpacking the entire AT seems completely impractical if not impossible. In fact, unless you have done a fair bit of research and planning, what is likely to come to mind first is how could one ever slackpack in the 100-Mile Wilderness, after all, isn't it supposedly an inaccessible "wilderness"?! Yet, when northbound thru-hikers reach Monson, ME, they will learn that among their options for getting through that famous stretch of the Trail is not just the possibility of food drops, but the potential of slackpacking some or all of it. Over the years a few shuttle services, most notably Poet at Shaw's Hostel, have developed relationships and permissions with the lumber companies whose roads crisscross the region creating not only food drop options but also slackpacking opportunities.

As audacious as it might sound to slackpack the 100-Mile Wilderness, perhaps, the purest form of platinum slackpacking we witnessed, however, was found in Gorham, NH where a young, female hiker used the gondola at Wildcat Mountain to break up the hike and slackpack through that portion of the Trail with just a daypack. First, she hiked from NH 16 to the gondola, rode the lift down to the resort and had Paul at Libby Barn pick her up. The next day she repeated this "lift-blazing" by hiking south from a spot north of the gondola, and then again riding the lift back down to the resort and another shuttle back to the hostel.

Chapter 4

HOW TO PLAN PLATINUM EXPERIENCES

Earlier in this guide we mentioned RTK's experience on the Camino de Santiago and his failure to take advantage of some of the special or iconic stops along the "way of St. James." The message, of course, is that better planning and preparation will help assure that anyone thru-hiking is less likely to miss the finest dining experiences, great hostels, iconic vistas, spectacular waterfalls, and "best" of everything else along the Trail.

Inevitably, a part of planning for platinum experiences is simply being prepared - reading ahead, knowing what to expect, and making plans. Fortunately, even when hiking during the peak (or "bubble") of AT thru-hike season, it is rarely as crowded as the Camino during peak summer months. However, like a good project planner, some consideration should still be given to making reservations if you are set on enjoying some of the best and most-popular AT experiences. This chapter is intended, therefore, to go beyond simply stressing planning and instead offer specific ideas and strategies to make Platinum-Blazing an integrated part of your AT experience.

Prepare Your Platinum Interests in Advance

One of the assumptions of this guide is that if you wait for the platinum experiences to present themselves, you will often pass them by. There are no flashing red lights pointing hikers off the Trail at critical junctures for a fine dining experience that may be nearby. For example, one of this book's editors and a member of what we lovingly call our "Platinum-Blaze Advisory Council" explained that he completely missed our Pure Platinum Award winner because he didn't realize what or where it was until he was miles north of it.

We recommend you study this guide well ahead of time and make your own notes and annotations to remind yourself of one or more of the platinum experiences that are most attractive to you. Then, as you refresh your planning, recall the platinum stops that are most important to you. Although planning out the whole hike in advance is not for everyone (and often shunned from purists), most everyone has a general idea of what they want to see or experience before they start. Let this be your guide for the best of the best!

Maximize the Value of your Platinum Stay.

By definition, a platinum stay is extra special – such as a private room at a fine bed & breakfast, or an upscale resort hotel. Anyone who travels much for a living knows that motel and hotel rooms can be a blur for the traveler who arrives late and departs early again the next morning. If a thru-hiker approaches town stays in the same manner, they should strongly consider whether staying at a place of fine lodging is appropriate – there simply is not enough time to justify the cost of the luxury accommodations. To be a true Platinum-Blazer, we think thru-hikers should plan to take a half-day (or "nero day") in the town where they plan on a platinum stay. A primary purpose of Platinum-Blazing is to add special experiences for rest and relaxation, and to recharge the emotional batteries by such a unique place. Simply put, a thru-hiker who shows up at a nice hotel at 8:00 p.m. and departs the next morning cannot possibly get all that is available at a platinum stop.

Double-Dip Platinum Activities

Often the impact of a platinum activity can be significantly enhanced by combining other, nearby Platinum-Blazing experiences. One way to think about these opportunities is to find two activities at the same location, and create a one plus one equals three opportunity. When you get more than one for the price of one (or double-dipping, as we call it), you will be taking full advantage of them all. The simplest and perhaps most common double-dip is to slackpack between two nights at luxury overnight accommodations. One who Platinum-Blazes in this fashion, we believe, gets exceptional value from the right-sized experiences that are grouped together.

Double-dipping could also be a complex string of platinum events. Such as, a nero day into town, stay at nice bed & breakfast, and then slackpack to the next overnight destination (which would involve meeting a shuttle driver with your gear or having it left at a safe place). Or, to explain specifically, nero into Hot Springs, stay at the Laughing Heart Lodge, have your backpack delivered to Hemlock Hollow hostel, while you hike north out of town with little or nothing on your back.

Another example of double-dipping, platinum activities to achieve a particularly valuable experience, is to simply take two nights at a luxury accommodation. We think if you're going to take a day off (or "zero day"), why not enjoy it somewhere where you have fine, private accommodations? Even more, why not stay somewhere with additional services, like access to a pool, hot tub, spa, fine dining room or even live theater. RTK spent two nights at a luxury accommodation in Damascus, called the Old Mill, specifically to have a private television for watching The Masters golf tournament. Another of RTK's double-dip, platinum stops was in Hot Springs, which he recounts below.

Perhaps my favorite platinum experience was combining a number of activities over two days in Hot Springs, NC. I hiked in and stayed at Elmer's Sunnybank Inn (with a private room). I enjoyed a special communal dinner with Ladybug, Stickers, Matt, and Elmer. The next day, I had Elmer's special breakfast with Eddie Steady, Rumi, Matt, and Elmer. After picking up my resupply box and collecting my laundry back from Elmer, I causally toured the town on a beautiful sunny, early spring day. I stopped by the Bluff Mountain Outfitters for fun, grabbed lunch at the Smoky Mountain Diner, walked to the resort and soaked in a natural hot springs' whirlpool bath, visited with fellow thru-hikers on the town streets and then met up with Scars for an exceptional lunch at the White Horse Tavern. After coffee, the next morning, I headed out a little after 7:00 a.m. I hiked across the French Broad River and out of town, feeling incredibly relaxed, refreshed and excited to continue the trek.

Because of the amenities it provides and the time during a thru-hike when people hit the town, Hot Springs can be a luxurious welcome for many early in their adventure. Sharkbait double-dipped a zero day by booking a 2-hour hot tub spa, followed by drinks and the special "AT Burger" at Spring Creek Tavern, and ending with a private heated cabin at the Hot Springs Resort along the river.

Another great place to combine platinum lodging and dining is in one of the most unlikely locations ... Port Clinton, PA. Some may tell you there is nothing luxurious for hikers in this old coal and anthracite mining town, except perhaps the Port Clinton Hotel. Although better than the open-air pavilion that most hikers sleep in for free, the Port Clinton Hotel has a reputation for treating hikers poorly. However, with a little planning and a little luck, you could enjoy one of the best double-dip experiences along the Trail in this small forgotten town. For Sharkbait, it was one of the most memorable days.

The hike leading into Port Clinton was rough. Multiple days of rain had turned the Appalachian Trail into a 10-foot wide and 6-inch deep river for miles on end. The growingly large and sharp rocks were also becoming a painful nuisance, so a day off and chance to rest comfortably was welcomed. I had read in AWOL's guide that a small bar called the Union House was open on the weekends, and sometimes had rooms to rent. The Union House is owned and operated by a local celebrity named Herm, who appears to own much of the small town (including 3 motorcycle sales and repair shops). Herm converted this small home into a side business in order to keep his Italian-trained culinary skills fresh for friends and family in town.

It was a Friday night around 6 pm when I walked up, and a dozen of Herm's close friends gathered on the front porch, waiting for him to arrive. Shortly later he did and I joined them in a night of drinking, storytelling, playing music, and dining on Herm's amazing menu. The food did not disappoint (nor did the cheap tap beers), and the live music made it an unforgettable experience. With a room just up the stairs, and a nero day to follow, it was exactly what my weary body and mind needed to recharge. And all in the same place!

With not much else besides an old-fashioned candy shop and barber (both excellent places to visit), Port Clinton is usually a quick pass-through town for hikers looking to get through rocky Pennsylvania as quick as possible. But, even rough areas of the Trail like this, have multiple Platinum-Blaze potential ... if timed right.

Practical Tips & Resources

Inevitably, the ability to not just enjoy, but maximize, your potential for Platinum-Blazing will require some advance planning. If done right, you will know when your own favorite platinum experiences are coming up on the Trail, and how to coordinate them. Reservations and timing may be necessary for some, planning in advance will help ensure nothing is missed. Keep this guide handy so that you can make all the arrangements necessary for a special side trip or important stop along the way. Even if you need not make reservations ahead of time, or even if you want to be more spontaneous about your hike (and platinum experiences), it will still benefit you significantly to have a guide like this with you.

If you'd rather not carry this guide with you, before departing for Springer (or Katahdin or elsewhere) ... we get it, every ounce on your back has to be calculated. However, you should at least use the following pages to record detailed notes about the platinum options that most interest to you. Including various of the stops and visits recommended here is likely to have a significant positive impact on you and help make your thru-hike extraordinary. You will want names, places, and activities - but as a practical matter, you will definitely need telephone numbers, physical addresses and email addresses.

Your Personal Concierge

Earlier in this chapter we mentioned how double-dipping platinum experiences could significantly enhanced your off-trail experience, by combining two or three activities in at once. Likewise, in the previous "Personal Concierge" chapter, we described the many ways a friend or assistant at home could make you a champion Platinum-Blazer by assisting with critical logistics such as resupply drops, reservations, shuttle arrangements, and the like. It should go without saying, but as a guide for planning "how to thru-hike in three-star luxury," we don't mind being obvious or redundant – you should also double-dip your preparation! Combine your use of a personal concierge with the many possible platinum experiences that are available. Because you had the foresight to equip your personal concierge with a copy of this book, he or she can help you understand when great opportunities are coming up ahead along the Trail, and can better help with execution by coordinating, suggesting alternatives and making reservations.

Closing Thoughts – A Word of Warning

Let us not sugarcoat it. After hiking for weeks on end, you will take on an appearance and an odor as a thru-hiker that will disgust most everyone with whom you come into contact. Your fellow thru-hikers will understand, but you will lose sight (and smell) of what passes as acceptable in society after a week of aggressive perspiration without shower. Hence, a challenge of every thru-hiker as they enter town, and particularly of those Platinum-Blazing, is recognizing the reaction you will receive from normal people. Most at a hostel will understand. Few at a fine restaurant or a 5-start bed & breakfast ever could.

Even a modest effort to clean yourself up will likely allow you (and others) to best enjoy the platinum opportunities outlined in this guide. And let's be honest, the proprietors appreciate it too! A sign in the dining room at the Port Clinton Hotel enjoins "Hikers Please shower Before Coming In to Eat." Similarly, the owner of the Old South Mountain Inn states "No sleeveless shirts. Please shower first" in AWOL's Guide.

The Knife Edge, Mt. Katahdin (from Baxter Peak)

Chapter 5

INTRODUCTION TO THE PLATINUM LISTINGS

With the foundation now laid on what Platinum-Blazing is, and how to best maximize your experiences while hiking he Appalachian Trail, the rest of this book provides a detailed guide for your planning convenience. In the chapters that follow, we highlight the individual listings of the very best luxury accommodations, premium hostels, meals, delis, pubs, breakfasts, waterfalls, and other not-to-be-missed special experiences along the Appalachian Trail that embody the Platinum-Blaze experience.

These "Platinum Listings" represent those experiences that we consider the most premium considerations. These are the elite of the elite and the most important must-see experiences for any Platinum-Blazer. Candidates for the Platinum Listings are not just our own opinions though; these represent a collection of winners from the feedback also collected from recent thru-hikers (especially our fellow 2018 thru-hiker class).

We believe these Platinum Listings provide a list of the Platinum-Blaze locations worthy for you to consider. In addition, for each category we identify a single "winner" that stands out as the best choice and identifying one stop along the AT we think is "too good to be missed" for that category. In the case of all of our selections, we believe a visit to those winners will forever be a special memory of your thru-hike.

Before going too far, it is worth calling out the elephant in the room … why is there a category for hostels? How could a hostel ever be considered luxury? At first glance you would be right, but the hostels we identified here are anything but Spartan and do in fact allow for 3-star luxury on the Trail. Even more, these hostels represent places where the owners/operators had a conscious and generous affection for the AT and attention to the needs of thru-hikers. Those attributes are important characteristics to consider, as they help create or add to the feel and "hiker-welcoming vibe" of the place. The hostels listed in this guide are indeed platinum-worthy and showcase locations that go above and beyond hostel normalcy. Those listed here typically offer platinum experiences, such as private accommodations, a high standard for cleanliness, and an array of premium amenities.

Additionally, when we considered a meal or a restaurant for the Platinum Listings, we took other considerations into effect, such as convenience and proximity to the Trail. RTK had an unplanned opportunity to enjoy a great meal in Banner Elk when staying in Roan Mountain, but we excluded that restaurant because it was over 20 miles away. On the other hand, Sharkbait discovered exceptional fine dining at Rocca Bar Ristorante in Lexington, VA when bypassing Buena Vista for the slightly further (but more upscale) college-town of Lexington in Virginia. Since either town would require a long ride from the US Road 60 trailhead, we did include Rocca Bar Ristorante here.

We typically tried to consider only restaurants within 10 miles of the Trail, as anything further would be logistically difficult to recommend. However, there are exceptions. The Inn at Little Washington is 15 miles from the AT and would normally not make our list, and while it was excluded from our "Best Platinum Restaurants" list, it is given special recognition due to its public recognition as a must-visit restaurant nationally.

This Guide also covers the very best side trips near the AT worth a visit. These experiences will take you to the best waterfalls, vistas, and other blue-blaze trails the AT offers. Finally, we also evaluate the best trail towns, city visits & unique destinations, and other special experiences along the Trail, which helps to introduce thru-hikers to some very special experiences that one can fit into their trek at certain locations with some simple planning.

Chapter 6

PURE PLATINUM AWARD

Before we review the Platinum Listings, we want to first highlight our overall winner, called the Pure Platinum Award. If we had to select just one off-trail visit to recommend as THE must-go experience along the Appalachian Trail, it would be **Woods Hole Hostel** in Giles County, Virginia, just ten Trail miles south of Pearisburg.

The Platinum Blaze Institute

Based upon input of the 2018 class of AT thru-hikers, and as published in *Platinum-Blazing the Appalachian Trail*, hereby recognizes:

Woods Hole Hostel

Pure Platinum Award

Best All-Around Luxury Accommodation & Trail Experience

Bruce "RTK" Matson

Michael "Sharkbait" Nisman

Founders and Authors of Platinum Blazing the Appalachian Trail

Operated by Neville near Pearisburg, VA, Woods Hole checks the box in almost every category we could think of. It has history, tradition, and significance to the Appalachian Trail hiking community. With a relaxed and inviting atmosphere, it provides countless services a hiker wants and needs for rest and recovery, including special communal meals with a focus on the familial experience.

The hostel dates back to 1986, when Neville's grandmother (Tillie Wood) invited the first smelly hikers to a stay at their family cabin. Even then the amenities were special, offering a "good old-fashioned southern breakfast of grits, eggs, sausage, gravy, jam, coffee, and juice for $3.50." The cabin was in Neville's family since 1939 as both a summer and permanent home for her family, but after Tillie died in 2007, Neville and Michael (who met in 2005 at Woods Hole during Michael's thru-hike) took over running the hostel, improving it every year since.

Woods Hole offers a bucolic setting – as they say, "on 100 acres of land, surrounded on three sides by the Jefferson National Forest and protected by 780 acres of privately-owned land in the foreground," and is just a reasonable 0.5 mile walk from the AT. Among the great joys of staying at Woods Hole is a welcoming milkshake when you arrive, group yoga sessions, or simply rocking on the porch of the main house and looking out over the exquisite property. RTK recalls Woods Hole in a very similar manner.

I had heard and read a lot about Woods Hole. I was eager to visit. The last couple of days leading up to the hostel, my lower back ached, so I decided to double-dip platinum activities for maximum recovery at Woods Hole. After a shuttle gathered me at Trent's Grocery, I arrived at the hostel and was greeted by my buddy Sharkbait and a number of other familiar thru-hiker faces. I checked into a private room, enjoyed one of Neville's famous massages, rocked peacefully on the front porch and relaxed before helping to prepare and then enjoy a communal meal, which was a wonderful gathering of Trail friends including Rumi & Eddie Steady, Professor, Sharkbait, Mouse Trap, Mom, Ridge, MacGyver, Soulshine, The Kid and Dragon.[1]

As stated on its website, Woods Hole emphasizes "sustainable living through organic farming, animal husbandry, communal meals, massage therapy, yoga, and much more." Thru-hikers can stay overnight in a cozy, clean and well-stocked bunkhouse, made of hand-hewn logs from the 1830s. Platinum-Blazers will be happy to learn that well-appointed, comfortable private rooms are also available. In fact, Woods Hole just completed the addition of new safari-style private "luxury tents" during the 2018 season, giving Platinum-Blazers another great reason to stay at this Pure Platinum experience. During a stay at Woods Hole hikers have the opportunity to assist in preparing the evening meal, consisting mostly of fresh ingredients from the property's organic farm.

Both of us stayed at Woods Hole in 2018 during our thru-hikes. In fact, we stayed there the same night and visited while enjoying the relaxing

---

[1] While writing this guide, we were devastated to hear that Matt "Dragon" Rossi died in a car accident shortly after completing his 2018 thru-hike. We both feel honored to have met him, known him, and hiked with him throughout Virginia.

chairs and scenic view from the porch of the main cabin. We helped prepare the evening meal and the community experience together. While RTK enjoyed his much-needed massage therapy, Sharkbait played music for friends on Neville's guitar. At the time RTK posted a photo of Woods Hole on his Instagram account, saying "No thru-hiker should pass up a stop here, simply the best. Thanks, Neville." Similarly, Sharkbait's daily blog that evening may as well have been a 5-star yelp review.

Bunkhouse at Woods Hole Hostel

[As we were going to print for this book, *The Hiker Yearbook* for 2018, produced by Odie came out. It was of little surprise to us that it featured a special recognition for Woods Hole Hostel. Much like our accolades for Neville and this special experience, Odie summarized Woods Hole simply as "a slice of heaven not to be missed."]

Chapter 7

PLATINUM OVERNIGHT ACCOMMODATIONS

When hikers want a warm bed and roof over their head for the night, there are many options to consider, depending on what is readily available nearby. This could include luxury hotels, resorts and lodges, hiker hostels, motels, or even a cozy Bed & Breakfast. Spending the night at a premium facility is the quintessential definition of Platinum-Blazing, as it provides a rare evening of luxury and respite from the weary trail.

Keep in mind that "luxury" is a relative term on the Appalachian Trail. As the subtitle of our guide suggests, 3-star luxury is usually the best you'll find for hiker accommodations. But, even 3 stars to an average vacationer can feel like 5 to an exhausted thru-hiker coming off multi-day tenting in the woods.

Platinum Hotels, Resorts and Lodges

The best luxury options on the AT are the rare but wonderful hotels, resorts and lodges that stand out as oases among the Howard Johnson and Motel 6 options often in trail towns. These premium locations are the best the Trail can offer and are surprisingly more common than you'd think. These resorts provide not just a great bedroom with an elegant private bathroom, but elite amenities such as pools, spas, restaurants, bars, or other activities to recharge one's emotional state as well. For Sharkbait, one place in particular was a highly-anticipated and long-awaited treat.

In pre-hike preparations, I knew the Allenberry Resort in Boiling Springs would be a must-stop accommodation. Previous hikers had given it glowing reviews, being well known as the only luxury resort with a live playhouse experience. Looking up the show schedule that year, I noted my trip in May would coincide with the stage production of Gypsy, so invited family to join me for the evening. A few weeks in advance, my personal concierge (my sister) booked a private cabin for the family on a weekend night, and I made it my mission to arrive on time. It was a hard push through rain and fog, but well worth the effort upon arrival. The restaurant, bar, theater, and cabin experience was one of the highlight moments of the entire trail. Future hikers beware though, weekends in May/June book up fast with weddings, school dances, and birthday parties ... in fact, we saw all 3 the night we were there.

Listing of Platinum Hotels, Resorts and Lodges on the AT

- **Amicalola Falls Lodge (Dawsonville, GA).** Unless you live close to the Trail, you'll likely need overnight accommodations near Amicalola Falls State Park. Start your hike by waking up in the mountains, where (as they say) "the clouds meet the earth". Breakfast is served starting at 7am at The Maple Restaurant, so you can start your thru-hike early at the Approach Trail's famous arch.

- **Fontana Dam Resort (Fontana Dam, NC).** This stunning mountain-side resort hosts a main hotel, private cabins, restaurant, bar, pool, laundry, and multiple stores for resupply and snacks. Fontana Dam is the only "town" that allows alcohol sales in Graham County, so enjoy a cold beer with your feet up on the gas fire-pit outside the main lodge while you witness the sun set over the Great Smoky Mountains.

- **Old Mill Inn (Damascus, VA).** This Inn is the only true hotel in Trail Town, USA. The rooms are spacious with beautiful, hardwood furnishings – nothing like standard Hilton or Marriott headboards and desks. Located on Laurel Creek at the former site of a grist mill, the inn's balconies overlook the mill pond and falls. A reasonable bar and good restaurant round out this property as a platinum stop.

- **Skyland & Big Meadows Lodges (Shenandoah National Park, VA).** Sure, you could use the communal shower-house/laundry room, visit the gift shop, or have a quick blackberry shake at the taproom before setting up your tent at a crowded campsite ... or, you could go platinum and book a private room at these beautiful lodges along Skyline Drive in Shenandoah National Park instead. Variable room options (and private cottages) are available, and all add luxury amenities to the standard campground facilities.

- **Allenberry Resort (Boiling Springs, PA).** In 2016, the Allenberry Resort came under new ownership. The playhouse that opened in 1949 was restored, comedy, drama and children's plays throughout the year. (Did you know, John Travolta acted there in the summer of 1971?). The restaurant on premise, The Barn, offers a wide range of delicious fare using seasonal farm-to-table ingredients and innovative flavors in a rustic chic setting.

- **Bear Mountain Inn (Bear Mountain, NY).** After hiking through Harriman Park and summiting Bear Mountain, thru-hikers can divert a hundred yards and spend the night at the Bear Mountain Inn, which offers luxurious rooms, a spa, and waterfront activities. The Hiker's Café offers quick snacks, or the Restaurant 1915 allows for sit-down dining (and a bountiful Sunday Brunch).

- **Berkshire Lakeside Lodge (Becket, MA).** If you decide not to stay at the beautiful Upper Goose Pond, which a Platinum-Blazer may well want to do, a lovely spot just 0.2E of the AT with nice rooms is the Berkshire Lakeside Lodge. True to its name, it sits on "88 acres of crystal-clear water of Greenwater Pond," on which you relax with the Lodge's canoes or kayaks. The Platinum-Blazer can also have Italian or Chinese food delivered.

- **Mountain Meadows Inn (Killington, VT).** On the shores of Kent Pond, this historic farmhouse and barn have been an institution of Vermont since 1857. The Inn took on new management with plans to re-open in the summer of 2019, but if the new owners remain hiker friendly, the cozy rooms, picturesque landscape, and relaxing atmosphere may be a future Pure Platinum winner.

- **Hanover Inn (Hanover, NH).** Few places to rest your head along the Trail cry out "Platinum!" upon first sight, but The Hanover Inn does. Nestled in the center of the Dartmouth College campus, you can treat yourself to elegant rooms, farm-to-table fine dining, and complimentary homemade cookies. In addition, the Hopkins Center for the Arts and Hood Museum are nearby for a leisurely zero-day activity.

- **Woodstock Inn (North Woodstock, NH).** What better time to treat yourself to exceptional accommodations than right after summiting the infamously iconic and treacherous Mt. Moosilauke? Thru-hikers can head six miles east to the Woodstock Inn, Station & Brewery for an exceptional room, pub, and breakfast that were also nominated in their respective award categories. Tour the brewery, experience the live entertainment, and relax for a day at one of the finest private lodging options anywhere along the Trail.

Best Platinum Hotel, Resort or Lodge:

Allenberry Resort
(Boiling Springs, PA)

A short, but uphill walk east off the Trail and just out of "downtown" Boiling Springs, is the acclaimed Allenberry Resort. This all-in-one lodge is without a doubt the very best luxury accommodation along the Appalachian Trail. With a recent ownership change, the rooms and common areas have all been refreshed and renovated. Time your visit well though, as (Sharkbait recaps above) it is a common destination for local events and celebrations

But even with a full crowd of party-guests, the resort provides respite from the Trail with all the amenities dreamed of. The rooms are impeccable, the restaurant exceptional, and the bar well-stocked with local spirits ... but the best part of the Allenberry Resort is the Playhouse, providing live theater on select nights. After an evening of fine dining and a showing of *Spamalot* (coming May 2019), you may find it a hard to walk the half-mile back to the trail in the morning.

Runners-Up:
- Bear Mountain Inn (Fort Montgomery, NY)
- Hanover Inn (Hanover, NH)

Up & Coming:
- Mountain Meadows Inn (Killington, VT)

Platinum Bed & Breakfasts

When resorts are unavailable, you don't need to return to an AT shelter. Just as common, if not more readily available along the Trail, are the charming and welcoming Bed & Breakfast locations. With their friendly hosts, family-style meals, and private guest bedrooms, you can find a luxury experience in a more familiar setting. Many B&Bs on the Trail are hiker-friendly, and although rooms can fill up fast during peak season (especially on weekends), they are great options to consider. For Sharkbait, these sometimes came at the most opportune time.

In May 2018, some may recall a quadruple tornado incident that pillaged the Hudson Valley, wreaking havoc on homes in NY, CT, and PA. It was scary to those watching the news in their homes, it was a nightmare for those sleeping in 3-walled shelters on the AT. After the nightmare ended, the aftermath was equally devastating. Trying to walk through Clarence Fahnestock State Park just days later was near impossible, as the tornado knocked out thousands of trees across the trail. With zero visibility and nonstop scrambling, arriving at Pawling a couple days later was like an oasis for the soul. Although guidebooks recommend the Dutchess Motor Lodge, I desperately needed a more platinum accommodation. I pulled out Google Maps and scanned the area for any B&B or upscale hotel. To my surprise, a new place showed that I had not seen in pre-hike planning, The Station Inn.

The owner (Susan) said the home was still under construction, but I could have my pick of the 2 finished rooms on the main level at a discount if I left before the workers arrived the next morning. I could not say yes fast enough, called an Uber from Dover Oak, and arrived to find what I now describe as a "Waldorf Astoria of the Moment." Nestled in the heart of downtown Pawling, the accommodations were incredible and exactly what I needed. My glowing review in Guthook that night must have been convincing, because RTK made his way there as well just a few weeks later.

Listing of Platinum B&Bs on the Appalachian Trail:

- **Misty Mountain Inn (Blairsville, GA).** While most thru-hikers will look for a bunk in the crowded Mountain Crossings at Neel gap, this B&B offers an Inn or private cabins just 15 minutes away (and comes with a free shuttle). The cabins are cottage-style, beautifully decorated and WiFi equipped, laundry is included with stay, and rides to and from town are easily arranged.

- **Nantahala Mountain Lodge (Franklin, NC).** Not to be confused with the Nantahala Outdoor Center (NOC), the NML is an exceptional choice for Platinum-Blazers a bit further south in North Carolina. The bunk room is "bunk less" with just five beds in the room, and the private rooms are upscale, bed & breakfast quality. NML also provides cooked breakfast and, upon request, a home-cooked dinner is available. Shuttles to and from the trail are provided and excellent slackpacking options are available.

- **Creekside Paradise B&B (Robbinsville/Fontana Dam, NC).** While most hikers stay at the Fontana Resort, Hike Inn, or Fontana Hilton prior to Great Smoky Mountain National Park, consider treating yourself at one of the nicest bed and breakfast inns on the Trail instead. Stop in and let Cynthia & Jeff recharge your emotional batteries before going on to tackle Clingmans Dome.

- **Elmer's Sunnybank Inn (Hot Springs, NC).** A truly unique place to stay, Elmer Hall offers up ancient hospitality traditions like those found in Taoist and Zen mountain inns since 1948. Hikers can slackpack from here for multiple nights and come back to gourmet organic vegetarian meals. Staffed by former hikers, this Inn provides "shelter, sustenance, and sanctuary to those who come our way."

- **Laughing Heart Lodge (Hot Springs, NC).** Absent careful attention, the thru-hiker may think Laughing Heart is just another hostel. It is a hostel, a very good hostel, but Laughing Heart also operates an exceptional lodge that offers massage, acupuncture and other healing therapies to its guests.

- **Roan Mountain B&B (Roan Mountain, TN).** A property that maintains the highest standards for any B&B. Owners Steve and Ann Campbell offer a remarkable option to the hiker community, and a perfect basecamp for slackpacking the Roan Highlands.

- **Mountain Harbour (Roan Mountain, TN).** Perhaps best known for its amazing family-style breakfast (read: banquet), Mountain Harbour also operates an excellent B&B on the same premises. Hikers can rent private rooms in the main house, or hostel-like beds in the converted barn. A food truck is also available most days for an extra treat.

- **Mountain Laurel Inn (Damascus, VA).** What better time to enjoy a premium stay than after reaching one of the greatest milestones of a thru-hike? Trail Town USA may host the raucous Trail Days, but when thru-hikers finally reach Virginia (having completed nearly ¼ of the journey), there are a number of opportunities to enjoy platinum accommodations. Mountain Laurel deserves special mention here, but careful consideration was given to Lazy Fox Inn, Dancing Bear B&B, and Dragonfly Inn as well - all of which offer wonderful hospitality and accommodations.

- **The Iris Inn (Waynesboro, VA).** Waynesboro is an exceptional trail town, and for someone looking to Platinum-Blaze, it would be hard to pass up a zero day at this mountaintop bed & breakfast. The views alone are worth the stay, but the rooms and breakfast are extraordinary as well. In addition, Waynesboro offers one of the nicest movie theaters along the Trail for a chance to take in the cinema.

- **Lily Garden B & B (Harper's Ferry, WV).** Within a block of the ATC headquarters on Washington Street in historic Harper's Ferry is Lily Garden B & B. This inn only has two private suites, but there will be little doubt you are Platinum-Blazing if you visit.

One suite has two bedrooms and the other is a large bedroom, so it may be better suited to a couple of Platinum-Blazers or that thru-hiker enjoying a visit from their spouse.

- **Rockhaven B & B (Harper's Ferry, WV).** Also close to the ATC headquarters is the lovely, Rockhaven B & B. Its location, like Lily Garden, makes walking the historic town very possible. This also has only two rooms, but both are elegant and provide a platinum experience.

- **Union House (Port Clinton, PA).** Just off Route 61 in Port Clinton, this bar and restaurant is only open on Fridays and Saturdays but provides one of the best combo destinations on the Trail. Hikers enjoy fine dining (made to order by Herm, the proprietor and an Italian-trained culinary chef), private beds to rent upstairs, and often live music among friends in the main taproom. Union House is less known, friendlier to hikers, and more eclectic than the Port Clinton Hotel a block away.

- **The Station Inn (Pawling, NY).** Although still under construction when both Sharkbait and RTK visited, the Station Inn could be a future favorite of many hikers once complete. Located off Main Street in downtown Pawling, these private rooms with smart televisions, WiFi and private bathrooms offer a comfortable place to relax and unwind for the night. In addition, the Pawling train station (also off Main Street) can take you directly to New York City.

- **Fife 'n Drum (Kent, CT).** An upscale Inn for an upscale town. Known for its proximity to a number of prep schools, Kent offers comfort and convenience to hikers … at a price. Nestled in the center of this cozy town, the Fife 'n Drum provides cozy beds, a gift shop, and a fine dining restaurant all in one place.

- **Reluctant Panther Inn (Manchester Center, VT).** This boutique inn bills itself as "Southern Vermont's Finest Small Luxury Hotel." And, it houses one of the top-rated restaurants in the state. It comes with a not surprisingly steep price tag, but then again, we're searching out the best platinum experiences along the Appalachian Trail.

- **The Sterling Inn (Caratunk, ME).** A gorgeous B&B with bunk or private rooms, a general store, continental breakfast, free laundry, WiFi, and shuttle rides around town. They don't have pulled pork sandwiches or milkshakes like the Caratunk House ... but they'll pick you up there for free after you've had your fill.

Best Platinum Bed & Breakfast:
Mountain Harbour B&B (Roan Mountain, TN)

When you walk up to Mountain Harbour B&B on Highway 19E, you immediately realize this place is special. Since 2003, Mary, David and Shannon have built what they call "an island to escape to that is surrounded by nothing but relaxing countryside". That statement could not be truer, as Mountain Harbour combines the aesthetic of a beautifully maintained hobby farm with the luxury of a modern mountain house. The Jefferson Room is as good as it gets, with its king-size four poster bed, built-in fireplace and private Jacuzzi tub. And all this, just a 0.3 mile walk from the trailhead.

Mountain Harbour is also host to a hiker hostel, whose accommodations and amenities rival that of even Woods Hole. This converted (or really, rebuilt) barn can only house a handful of hikers in the fully furnished loft, but the main floor lounge and kitchen provide everything else you need for a welcoming stay. In addition, the barn is host to a general store that sells everything a thru-hiker needs and wants for full resupply, and a fully operational food-truck of hot eats for those that don't partake in the B&B family-style meals.

But where Mountain Harbour really shines, is its communal breakfast in the main house. Whether you stay at the B&B or hostel, don't skip out on this treat, as it is one of the best breakfasts along the entire Appalachian Trail. Homemade biscuits and gravy, pancakes, sausages, fresh fruit, pastries, and a heavenly dish of pierogi scrambled eggs you won't want to miss.

Just sitting on the porch in the pleasant country setting is a platinum experience; but combining breakfast, slackpacking, and a private room here represents one of our favorite double-dipping platinum opportunities.

Runners-Up:
- Creekside Paradise B&B (Fontana Dam, NC)
- Roan Mountain B&B (Roan Mountain, TN)
- Union House (Port Clinton, PA)

Up & Coming:
- Station Inn (Pawling, NY)

Special Consideration. One final note on B&Bs. After Pawling, NY the platinum-minded, northbound thru-hiker could theoretically spend every night at a B&B and Platinum-Blaze all the way to the White Mountains … we call this the New England B&B Challenge. Check out the full New England B&B Challenge itinerary in the Appendix.

Shaw's Hiker Hostel

Green Mountain Hostel

Platinum Hostels

The last category for platinum lodging on the AT is Hostels. Stopping in at one of the many hostels that dot the Trail from Georgia to Maine is something almost every thru-hiker does on occasion, if not frequently. However, as we've already explained, it is difficult to call *any* hostel "luxury" by definition. A Platinum-Blazer will typically bypass the local hiker hostel for a nice B&B or hotel room instead. Yet, the hostel system is a cultural part of the thru-hiker community, and some owners fortunately recognize the opportunity to go above and beyond. We wanted to both recognize those exceptional facilities and their owners as well as providing some guidance to hikers on which stops they may want to make during their trek.

The quality of amenities, range of services, and choice of room options to hikers are almost as varied as the facilities that line the Trail. To be considered in the platinum listings for this category though, the hostel must provide more premium services, such as family-style meals, slackpacking, on-site resupply, and cleanliness. One factor pointing towards a platinum stay is the availability of private rooms within the hostel itself. (In this guide's Appendix, we identify the Best Private Accommodations at a Hostel.) As a general rule ...the more of these services it offered, the more desirable the hostel becomes:

- A complimentary "welcome" beverage
- Dinner offered for a charge (or no additional charge)
- A well-equipped kitchen provided for hiker use
- Breakfast offered for a charge (or no additional charge)
- Free breakfast supplies for DIY pancakes, etc.
- Availability of complimentary coffee, tea and hot chocolate
- Supply of first aid items, vitamin I, etc.
- Shoe glue, repair items, use of basic tools to assist with repairs
- Laundry facilities (preferably with soap provided or available)
- Loaner clothes provided for use while doing laundry
- Shuttle runs to and from the trailhead
- Shuttle runs to and from town for evening meals and for resupply
- Slackpacking services available
- Fresh linens & towels provided with bed/bunk

- Beds without bunks
- High-speed and reliable WiFi (capable of video streaming or uploading)
- Willingness to receive & hold mail drops securely
- Postal supplies & package delivery services
- On-site store selling food or gear resupply items
- On-site store selling cold drinks & hot snacks (e.g. pizza & ice cream)
- Comfortable community space indoors for relaxing (with television, book & video library, internet computer, etc.)
- Comfortable community space outdoors for relaxing (with chairs, fire pit, picnic table, outdoor grill, clothesline, etc.)
- All services offered with a generous and helpful spirit creating a relaxed atmosphere or "vibe"

A thru-hiker that is Platinum-Blazing should expect a great number of these premium services AND a high degree of helpful, quality service. (Sharkbait and RTK experienced every one of the items detailed above, but not at a single hostel.) This is a very high standard for a hostel owner to meet when attempting to provide such services for $20 to $40 per night. Accordingly, not all hostels make the list ... but we do hope they try to for the future!

Listing of Platinum Hostels on the Appalachian Trail:

- **Nantahala Mountain Lodge (Franklin, NC).** We identified Nantahala Mountain Lodge in the B & B category above. NML is also an exceptional choice for Platinum-Blazers seeking an exceptional hostel. The bunk room is "bunk less" with just five beds in the room. NML also provides cooked breakfast for hostel guests. Shuttles to and from the trail are provided and excellent slackpacking options are available.

- **Quarter Way Inn (Ceres, VA).** Owned and operated by Chunky (2009 SOBO thru-hiker), this exceptional hostel just north of Atkins, VA opened in 2015 and features include an eclectic country setting, a "bunk less" bunkroom, community common space, a tree swing, resupply, slackpacking, and exceptional breakfast.

- **Woods Hole Hostel (Giles County, VA).** It should be obvious, as Woods Hole is the winner of the Pure Platinum Award (described in Chapter 6), but we note Woods Hole's inclusion in this list of the very best hostels along the Appalachian Trail. If you stay nowhere else on the AT, stay at Woods Hole.

- **Bear's Den (Northern Virginia).** Just off the Trail in the middle of the "Roller Coaster," this stop has a great atmosphere and offers perhaps the best "deal" on the AT: $30 for a bunk, laundry, pizza, cold drink, and a pint of Ben & Jerry's ice cream).

- **Rock 'n Sole Hostel (Summit Station, PA).** Rock 'n Sole is a fairly new entry to the list of AT hostels, having just opened in 2016. At first glance, it seems passable - a fairly small bunkhouse with adequate bathroom facilities (outdoor shower, chemical toilet), but within thirty minutes you can see that Craig and Jody have worked hard to make every aspect of this hostel practical, useful, and welcoming. Other amenities include free hot drinks, ice cream and snacks for sale, laundry w/loaner clothes, slackpacking available, and private accommodations in a vintage camper. Jody's exceptional breakfast and dinner are included with your overnight stay.

- **Bearded Woods Bunk & Dine (Sharon, CT).** Owned and operated by thru-hikers Hudson & Big Lu since 2012, Bearded Woods provides all the essential services needed, plus a nice complimentary breakfast. Consider a free slackpack with 2-night stay or enjoy the great outdoor space and comfortable common areas for a zero day.

- **Green Mountain House (Manchester Center, VT).** Green Mountain is one of the truly amazing hostels on the AT. Some thru-hikers may claim Manchester Center is too "bougie" for a stop, but things that might be bougie to many thru-hikers are attractive to Platinum-Blazers.

- **The Notch Hostel (North Woodstock, NH).** An exceptional hostel along the Trail that offers private accommodations and an almost-perfect list of premium services. In fact, evaluating The Notch's catalog of services helped us create the template for reviewing all hostels. Located after Mt. Moosilauke with access to North Woodstock and Lincoln, yet The Notch provides most of the comfort and services needed on site.

- **Rattle River Lodge & Hostel (Gorham, NH**). Incredibly positioned right on the Trail after finishing the White Mountains, this hostel provides a great stop before tackling the tough mountains of southern Maine. An excellent array of services are provided, including a large communal kitchen & dining room, many slackpacking options and fun outdoor activities space (including a tiny pond with boats). Private rooms are available, such as the Franklin Room, which wins our award for finest private room at any hostel.

- **Hiker Hut (Rangeley, ME).** In fairness, there is nothing luxury about this stop off Maine's Highway 4. The only option outside of the bunk-house is 1 of 2 private (and very small) cabins. There is no electricity or plumbing, but the Hiker Hut makes up for this with character. This sanctuary of tranquility rests along the Sandy River, hosting flower gardens, hummingbirds, and pet (yes, pet) chipmunks. Other amenities include snacks on arrival, pastries on departure, hot meals, laundry, rides to town, fresh linens, and a licensed sports massage therapist on premise.

- **Shaw's Hiker Hostel (Monson, ME).** This iconic and tenured hostel welcomes you to recharge before venturing into Maine's 100-Mile Wilderness. Serving thru-hikers for over 40 years, Shaw's Hiker Hostel is now run by 2008 thru-hikers Poet & Hippie Chick. There may not be another hostel that offers the array of services available at Shaw's, where in addition to tenting, bunk and private room options, there is a full outfitter, large resupply, outdoor space, Poet's now famous breakfast (also featured on our list of "Best Breakfasts"), and easy access to town (Monson). And, of special note, food drop options for the 100-mile Wilderness.

Best Platinum Hostel:

Green Mountain House
(Manchester, VT)

With Woods Hole already winning the overall Pure Platinum Award, this award goes to the next runner-up. Green Mountain Hostel, however, is no after-thought and is very deserving of both this award and your visit.

Green Mountain Hostel is a home in the outskirts of the tourist town of Manchester Center, Vermont. Owned and operated by Jeff & Regina Taussig (Jeff completed a section hike of the AT in 2006), this hostel helped set the standards for the quality, type and breadth of accommodations and services most responsive to the needs (and wishes) of thru-hikers. In addition to opening his home to hikers, Jeff has stayed closely connected to the AT community and developed the idea of the now popular "AT Passport." Here's RTK's take on Green Mountain Hostel:

Initially, I was turned off by what I read in the AWOL Guide: "Hitchhike to town and then we'll pick you up". It's hard to think of hitchhiking as being part of a platinum experience. I excluded a visit from my original plans. As I hiked into Vermont a very seasoned thru-hiker and highly knowledgeable Trail personality urged me to go see Jeff and stay at GMH. I valued the source and changed my plans and I'm so happy I did. Essentially, GMH has everything a hostel could have, including a welcoming and helpful vibe. When establishing a catalog of the services indicative of a "best" hostel, we started with everything I saw and experienced at GMH first.

As RTK suggested, Green Mountain offers just about anything a thru-hiker wants and is well suited to welcome Platinum-Blazers. There are well-supplied and extraordinarily clean bathroom facilities, free laundry supplies and equipment (and loaner clothes), relaxing common spaces equipped with computer terminal, piano, guitar, and a video library, excellent private rooms, a well-stocked kitchen open for use by hikers at any time (including supplies for free, "cook-your-own" breakfast, mailing and package delivery services, and outdoor space with grill, picnic table and clothes line). And, if that's not enough, Ben & Jerry's pints are sold for $1!

Runners-Up:
- The Notch Hostel (Glencliff, NH)
- Shaw's Hiker Hostel (Monson, ME)

Up & Coming:
- Human Nature Hostel (Andover, ME)
- Station 19 (Roan Mountain, TN)
- Hostel of Maine (Carrabassett Valley, ME)

Breakfast at Rock 'n Sole Hostel

Chapter 8

PLATINUM MEALS & TOWN FOOD

There may be no more prevalent reason for getting off the trail than to indulge in real food, even more than the need for resupply (although both are often found at the same). The cravings for hot food come long before the infamous hiker hunger of insatiable appetites, as seen by how many $10 frozen pizzas Mountain Crossings sells annually at Neel Gap just 4 days in.

In a more specific example, one day RTK was hiking with a group of 20-year olds when he noticed one of the young hikers run ahead of the group. Upon reaching his campsite for the night, he found out why ... the fast hiker wanted to arrive early enough to set up his tent, empty his pack, and hike a few more miles to a McDonalds. It may sound crazy to a casual hiker (or pending first-time thru-hiker), but those half-dozen miles equated to thirty hamburgers for the crew, a treat they all cherished.

It's common for many thru-hikers to walk between 0.5 and 1.0 miles every day (especially in NY/NJ) to find a meal that isn't pre-packaged or days old in your pack. When Sharkbait stopped in Pawling, he walked 4 miles back to the Station Inn from dinner, just so he could indulge in the highly recommended Big W's Roadhouse BBQ. The stories of thru-hikers taking special if not extraordinary steps for a burger or a pizza or a deli sandwich are legion, if not legend.

The slight problem to rating restaurants on the Trail, however, is that they are heavily skewed by the mere fact you've been deprived of fresh ingredients for so long. Due to the typical thru-hiker meals on the trail (and frequent calorie deficit), thru-hikers embellish how grand town meals really are. Average meals are rated "very good" and good meals are thought of as "exceptional". As a result, and not to disparage these fine establishments, there tends to be a bit of grade inflation when it comes to rating a restaurant or a meal on the Trail. There's nothing wrong with this, as thru-hikers do spend a lot of time depriving themselves of that type of treat … but casual hikers may have different opinions to those here.

For example, although thru-hikers rave about Daniel's Steakhouse in Hiawassee, GA and Ming Garden in Waynesboro, VA … these places do not have "great" food. What they do have is a lot of food at a modest price, which is why they are so popular and famous among hikers. The number of truly excellent or exceptional restaurants is actually quite small, and because Platinum-Blazers have a taste for the finer things, we have listed the "Best Restaurants" based more on quality than quantity or value. However, due to their popularity on the Trail, we did identify the best of these value restaurants below as well.

To distinguish between what hikers desire most, we categorized town food by specific type. In this chapter, you'll find our platinum-listings broken out by Best Restaurants, Best Breakfast, Best Ice Cream, Best Brewery/Pub, Best Deli, Best Burger, Best Pizza, and Best Value Restaurant.

Platinum Restaurants

It is well-known that thru-hikers suffer a calorie deficit almost every day on the Trail. Some estimates suggest that sojourners along the AT burn on average 5,000 – 8,000 calories each day but consume only about half that amount. And although pizza or burgers may be the most sought-after food when thru-hikers get to town, there are some great options to sit down and have a fine dining experience on the Trail.

With a little planning, one can have some truly platinum experiences dining along the Trail. As mentioned, replacing the usual Ramen noodles and Knorr sides for anything is a much-needed emotional recharge, but doing so with a parmesan-crusted Dover sole or NY strip steak with an appropriate wine pairing is a special treat. For both RTK and Sharkbait, luxury was found in a well-prepared plate of veal or chicken parmigiana. RTK recounts:

> *I went into Roan Mountain, TN for the Easter weekend. I heard from Scars that he too was in town. The owner of Station 19 agreed to run us up to Banner Elk. Before I knew it I felt like we were about as far from the Trail as possible, in a fine Italian restaurant with a fine bottle of Chianti. After a Caesar salad the main course arrived, I snapped a photo of my favorite meal and texted my wife: "What's for dinner? It's not a Trailtopia freeze-dried pack tonight."*

Because of the unique nature of these fine-dining experiences, our listings include locations within reasonable proximity to a trailhead and with access to transportation. For purposes of this chapter, we define that as less than 10 miles away and on a main road. For example, if the restaurant requires hiking 3 miles down a side trail, and another 5 along a private logging road, it would not make the list. Additionally, if the restaurant is more than 10 miles by car (like The Inn at Little Washington of Virginia) it too was excluded. [2]

Listing of Platinum Restaurants on the Appalachian Trail:

- **Bodensee (Helen, GA).** Chef Aurel Prodan studied at a culinary school in Romania before bringing this authentic German cuisine to an American alpine village. The widely popular recommendation is the Jaegar Pork Schnitzel with mushroom cream sauce.

---

[2] Although we do recommend a visit to The Inn at Little Washington located in Little Washington, Virginia (see our list of "The Best City Visits & Unique Side Trips near the AT" below), it is approximately fifteen miles from Thornton Gap on the AT.

- **Caffé Rel (Franklin, NC).** Situated in an old gas station, this local favorite is often crowded but worth the stop. Rosemary Infused Gruyere Mac and Cheese ... need we say more?

- **River's End (Nantahala Outdoor Center, NC).** The NOC's accommodations may leave you wanting, but the riverside restaurant at this outdoor recreation center will not. The always fresh trout cake sandwich is a good option, but really anything served with those mouth-watering French fries will do.

- **Iron Horse Station (Hot Springs, NC).** Although most hikers will head straight to the Spring Creek Tavern upon arrival to this favorite trail town, save room for an elegant steak dinner and chocolate peanut butter pie at this historic haberdashery building.

- **Mojo's Trailside Cafe (Damascus, VA).** The trail town of Damascus leaves much to be desired for a Platinum-Blazer, but it does have its gems and Mojo's is such a place. Although a small coffee shop vibe, the menu is robust and worth a stop. It doesn't hurt that this is one of the only places in town that serves alcohol. Don't leave without sampling a homemade cinnamon roll.

- **Old Mill (Damascus, VA).** Featuring a classic dining, relaxing pub, and three outdoor decks overlooking a private waterfall, Old Mill is another reason not to rush to a hostel like Crazy Larry's when you arrive. In fact, Old Mill is the only full-service hotel and restaurant in Damascus.

- **Rocca Bar Ristorante (Lexington, VA).** Located on the 2nd floor of the Robert E. Lee Hotel with a stunning backdrop of the Blue Ridge Mountains. You'll forget you are a thru-hiker for the evening as you enjoy this Italian fine dining experience. By now on your thru-hike, you could spend a week's worth of budget filling up on this one meal ... but it would be worth it.

- **Old South Mountain Inn (Boonsboro, MD).** Located next to Dahlgren campground near Turner's Gap, but servicing tourists coming to see Antietam Battlefield, Washington Monument State

Park, Harpers Ferry and Gambrill State Park. Perhaps the only place to pair a delicious Lobster Bisque appetizer with Scallops Provencal. Don't rule out the Beef Wellington though. In fact, picking just one elegant meal here may be tough.

- **Blue Mountain Summit (Andreas, PA).** This old English style pub is uniquely located to give hikers a grand meal when they need it most. Grab some Yuengs and Wings (which is a nod to Yuengling - Pennsylvania's famous and the country's oldest brewery) for lunch before taking on Pennsylvania's infamous Bake Oven Knob and Knife's Edge.

- **Union House (Port Clinton, PA).** Mentioned earlier, for those lucky enough to arrive on a Friday or Saturday, Herm will cook you up anything your heart desires. His menu is extensive, his culinary skills are unquestionable, and his meals are exquisite. You'd never expect such a dining experience in this small tavern/B&B.

- **Boiling Springs Tavern (Boiling Springs, PA).** Specializing in classic American fare with a modern twist, the menu includes a wide selection of steaks, seafood and pastas, accompanied by an extensive wine list and craft beer selection.

- **Deer Head Inn (Delaware Water Gap, PA).** You'll want need a good meal after getting through "Rocksylvania". Dinner is only served Thursday through Sundays and select Mondays at this oldest continuously running jazz club in the country. For a real treat, go for the Jazz Package and get dinner, music, a room for the night, and breakfast the following morning.

- **Sycamore Grill (Delaware Water Gap, PA).** Another option in DWG, with great hiker deals and daily specials (and a reasonably good bar). It will be tough to choose between the chicken & broccoli sacchettini or Wagyu Kobe beef hamburger, but you really can't go wrong with anything on the menu.

- **McKinney & Doyle (Pawling, NY).** Located right across the street from the train station, there is no need for a trip to NYC to get a good meal in Pawling. The bakery and coffee shop are reason alone to stop, but the fine-dining menu is extensive and outstanding.

- **Plated Modern American Bistro (Fishkill, NY).** Just 5 miles north from RPH Shelter along the Taconic State Parkway. Although the menu is filled with great Italian fare, Mike's Famous Chicken parmigiana may be the best meal on the trail.

- **Fife 'n Drum Restaurant (Kent, CT).** You really can't go wrong with any of the restaurants in Kent, but this is the premier dining choice for those wishing an elegant all-around dining experience.

- **Water Street Grill (Williamstown, MA).** If you put this book down for a minute, and navigate to their website (waterstgrill.com), the rotating picture carousel of menu items is all the review you need. After descending from Mt. Greylock, celebrate the completion of the AT in Massachusetts by heading west for a meal. Less than 3 miles to the center of Williamstown (and Williams College), this mainstay is where locals direct their visitors – even smelly thru-hikers.

- **Mulligan's Restaurant & Pub (Manchester Center, VT).** Mentioned earlier, this off-trail gem has the best Applewood smoked chicken wings around. Getting to town will take a shuttle or hitch, and getting to Mulligan's from where you are staying will take another ride but sitting outside on the patio for these award-winning wings is worth the extra cost for a ride.

- **Molly's (Hanover, NH).** Depending on when you arrive, Dartmouth College can be overrun with visitors for graduation and alumni events. But for those lucky enough to avoid the crowds, or willing to wait, a stop at Molly's is worth the effort.

- **Libby's Bistro & SAalt Pub (Gorham, NH).** When Liz Jackson moved home, Coös County's only culinary claim to fame was a teacher who supposedly invented the casserole in 1866. Not anymore. Liz learned to cook at the Cambridge School of Culinary Arts, then spent 2 summers cooking alongside Julia Child. Both the meal and the dishes they are served on are crafted by her hands, and provide an incredible treat for anyone, let alone AT thruhikers.

- **Mr. Pizza (Gorham, NH).** With a name like Mr. Pizza, it is hard to believe this is worth a stop, but it is. Its menu is considerably broad, including salads, American favorites and even seafood. (RTK had fried, "whole-belly" clams – a delicacy he craves from his youth in New England.) We definitely recommend Libby's above over Mr. Pizza, but if you take a zero day in Gorham like most hikers do, be sure to dine-in here as well.

- **White Wolf Inn (Stratton, ME).** Serving up giant "wolf" burgers and "down home" turkey pot pie, Chef Sandi Isgro promises to satisfy every hearty hiker appetite. The dining room is anything but elegant, but with menu items like lemon cream drizzled lobster stuffed haddock wrapped in smoked salmon, we think the food is worth it.

- **Sarge's Sports Pub & Grub (Rangeley, ME).** A great sports pub in the center of this gorgeous Maine mountain town. If a bar scene is not your style, instead check out the Hungry Trout at the Saddleback Inn further south on Main Street. Both pair equally well with dessert at the Pine Tree Frosty.

- **Lakeshore House (Monson, ME).** Although not the best hostel in Monson (see Shaw's), the restaurant is exquisite. Grab a table in the back for a beautiful view of Lake Hebron, adorned with eclectic Appalachian Trail artwork.

20 19

Best Platinum Restaurant:

Caffé Rel (Franklin, NC)

Neither Sharkbait nor RTK visited every one of our platinum "winners." The extraordinary experience offered by Caffe Rel came to our attention from a number of our fellow, 2018 thru-hikers. In particular, our thanks to Paul "Seven" Castillo for his assistance in preparing this write-up of our selection here. Built into the side of a gasoline station, Seven calls a meal at Caffé Rel as "Premium Fuel." Consistent with the remarks we heard, one magazine review said this:

> *As soon as you sit down, a dish of welcome arrives: Caffé Rel's tomato bruschetta delivers thick olive oil infused with chopped herbs, garlic, and crushed tomatoes, and generous hunks of baguette for dunking. Consider this the preview to a meal filled with robust and rustic flavors, wonderful French classics that you don't typically experience in a small mountain town.*

This exceptional restaurant serves classic French (think savory sauces) and Italian dishes. You won't find it in any of the traditional thru-hiker guides, and most hikers only find their way past the fuel pumps to Chef Richard Long's door due to the urging of locals. Among the featured items are Crab Bisque, Coquille St. Jacques, and Crawfish Cognac & Cream, but you can also enjoy some more basic items such as mac 'n cheese, shrimp and grits, Italian subs or a lamb burger. Locals insist you order the chocolate cake (tall and layered), inspired by the chef's Belgian mother.

And, perhaps best of all for the thru-hiker, its premium fare at bistro prices. Although a clear platinum experience, there are some drawbacks to consider: only open four days a week, no reservations, no

72

place to wait and no credit cards accepted. As Seven told us, "make the effort to get into Franklin, and come hungry to Caffé Rel."

Runners-Up:
- McKinney & Doyle – Pawling, NY
- Iron Horse Station (Hot Springs, NC)
- Libby's Bistro & SAalt Pub (Gorham, NH)

Honorable Mention:
- Old South Mountain Inn (Boonsboro, MD)
- Water Street Grill (Williamstown, MA)

Platinum Breakfasts

Below is our list of the very best places on or near the AT for breakfast. There is an excellent variety here, including great classics like the family-style breakfast provided by Paul "One Braid" Fuller at Caratunk House and the remarkable "eggs-to-order" with special house fries and blueberry pancakes turned out by Poet at Shaw's Hiker Hostel. The list includes a nod to Jody at Rock 'n Sole for her exceptional cooking, a few traditional restaurants like Looney Moose Café and Up for Breakfast, and a couple of unique breakfast experiences like Harrison's Pierce Pond Camp and White House Landing.

Listing of Platinum Breakfasts on the Appalachian Trail:

- **Roan Mountain B&B (Roan Mountain, TN).** The way breakfast should be – attentive personal service, everything to order and more than enough to eat. Ann changes it up or provides whatever you request the second or third morning.

- **Mountain Harbour B&B/Hostel (Roan Mountain, TN).** As already mentioned in the Best Hostels section, Mountain Harbour's breakfast is worthy even for those who don't spend the night. Sharkbait's dreams for days after were often filled with those pierogi scrambled eggs.

- **Quarter Way Inn (Ceres, VA).** Homemade honey, apple butter, blackberry jam, cheesy grits and more greet you at this gourmet trail breakfast near Marion and Atkins, VA.

- **Woods Hole (Giles Country, VA).** You already know Woods Hole is our top all-around choice, but it's worth reminding not to leave before breakfast. Unlike the family-style dinner, breakfast is plated and served to you by the friendly staff, but using the same home-grown ingredients and delicious recipes that make Woods Hole amazing.

- **Rock 'n Sole Hostel (near mile 1199 in Summit Station, PA).** A truly homemade breakfast with potato casseroles, fruit, juice, coffee, egg casseroles, and amazing coffee cake served up on the porch of Jody's home. So good, it's hard to believe it is included with the cost of a stay.

- **Toymaker's Café (Falls Village, CT).** A popular, local favorite, expect a line for an open table. But one smell of the cinnamon butter waffle and you'll be more than willing to wait.

- **Up for Breakfast (Manchester Center, VT).** This Vermont mountain town is more populous than most stops along the Appalachian Trail, so there is no shortage of options for your morning fill-up. But don't be tempted by the Starbucks and Dunkin' Donuts in town, and instead make your way to this local favorite for The Hungry Hiker or the Morning Glory Pancakes (cinnamon based batter filled with coconut, raisins, pineapple, carrots, apple & nuts).

- **Looney Moose Café (Stratton, ME).** With a goal to make everyone that enters their doors feel that they "just walked into their best friend's house", the Looney Moose will feel like home. Fresh ingredients, hearty meals, and seasonal favorite make this a favorite stop for Sugarloaf Mountain visitors.

- **Caratunk House B&B/Hostel (Caratunk, ME).** This family-style, communal feast of almost unlimited eggs, fruit, bacon, and more served up by Paul is a required stop along the Trail.

- **Harrison's Pierce Pond Camp (0.3E of Pierce Pond shelter; south of Caratunk, ME)**
  A visit to this classic, yet dusty, Maine hunting camp is rewarded by Tim Harrison's wonderful hospitality and a pancake breakfast to remember. The beautiful, short hike by some falls at the outlet of Pierce Pond is an extra bonus.

- **Shaw's Hiker Hostel (Monson, ME).** We don't really need to tell you to stay at Shaw's, because just about every hiker will. But we will remind you not to skip Poet's legendary breakfast. With pyramids of blueberry pancakes, home fries, and more greasy bacon than imaginable, this is the fuel you need to enter the 100-mile wilderness.

- **White House Landing Wilderness Camp (100-Mile Wilderness, ME).** For those needing a break from the 100-Mile Wilderness, this is your stop. A traditional camp breakfast of bacon, eggs, orange juice, coffee, English muffins and all-you-can-eat blueberry pancakes in a fabulous setting. Just 30 miles from Baxter State Park.

> ## Best Platinum Breakfast:
> ### Quarter Way Inn (Ceres, VA)

The Quarter Way Inn is a hostel run by Tina "Chunky" Tempest, a 2009 thru-hiker, which also made our "best of" list for hostels along the AT (see Chapter 7). Located just north of Atkins, as its name suggests, The Quarter Way Inn is near the 25% completion mark for NOBO hikers. RTK and Sharkbait had a long debate, but in the end, Quarter Way defeated Mountain Harbour for Best Platinum Breakfast on the Trail. Quarter Way is relatively new (opened in 2015) and therefore less known, but that won't last long as word of this gem travels among future hikers. More importantly, in the quality category, there was no contest. Mountain Harbour has an exceptional breakfast, but here at the Platinum-Blaze, we thought the Quarter Way Inn inched it out due to Tina's care, creativity and quality.

Breakfast costs just $12.00, consisting of jalapeño cheese biscuits, pimento cheese grits, a broccoli egg casserole, cinnamon coffee cake, bacon, a variety of fresh fruit, teas, juices, coffee and more. Special to

Quarter Way is the homemade apple butter, locally-farmed honey, and blackberry preserves made on site. For those familiar with traditional southern home-style cooking, you'll appreciate a good biscuit. Simply stated, these biscuits were the finest RTK has ever eaten. Additionally, why no one else thought to make pimento cheese grits before is beyond our knowledge, but they are simply extraordinary here. In RTK's words, "during your thru-hike, you should visit Tina at the Quarter Way Inn for an evening and the best breakfast on the Appalachian Trail."

Runners-Up:
- Mountain Harbour B&B/Hostel
- Up for Breakfast (Manchester Center, VT)
- Shaw's Hiker Hostel (Monson, ME)
- Looney Moose (Stratton, ME)

Honorable Mention:
- Timbers (Fayetteville, PA)
- Welsh's (Gorham, NH)

The Quarter Way Inn

Platinum Ice Cream/Milkshakes

Cravings for ice cream on the Trail, like pizza and burgers, are often influenced more by deprivation than the quality of offering. After two weeks hiking in the rain and rocks of Pennsylvania, Sharkbait was ready to crown a Burger King chocolate shake as the best meal on the Trail. For RTK, he swears one of the best pizzas came from a gas station. Considering these two memories, we thought identifying the best ice cream on the AT was a fool's errand. There are simply too many types, too many individual preferences, and too many purveyors to list a top 10.

But, like pizza and burgers, ice cream has a special place in a thru-hiker's heart. It is among the most sought-after food when hikers reach town. It's rare to come across ice cream trail magic (though we did see it done), so we thought this trail favorite deserved its own "best of" list.

Before we reveal that list, however, we want to recognize and dedicate this section to Bill Ackerly ("The Ice Cream Man"), one of the AT's great trail angels, who greeted thru-hikers for years by offering them ice cream bars (and a place to tent) at his home in Lyme Center, NH. Certainly, one of the disappointments of our thru-hikes in 2018 was not being able to enjoy the platinum experience of visiting with The Ice Cream Man, who sadly passed away during the 2016 hiking season.

Listing of Platinum Ice Cream/Milkshakes on the Appalachian Trail:

- **Waysides in Shenandoah National Park (VA).** Not quite the same quality of milkshake as the Caratunk House offers, but the waysides in Shenandoah National Park offer iconic blackberry milkshakes that no thru-hiker should bypass.

- **South Mountain Creamery (Middletown, MD).** Fresh, local, farm-to-table ice cream at this family-owned dairy farm, which also offers a variety of fresh eggs, cheese, milk butter and other farm products – well worth the 2-mile Uber.

- **Pine Grove Furnace General Store (Pine Grove Furnace State Park, PA).** Simple, average-quality carton ice cream. But the atmosphere, culture and history as the home of the half-gallon challenge, makes a stop here imperative. Sharkbait recommends Hershey's Black Raspberry.

- **Sweet Nanny's (Wind Gap, PA).** Before tackling the last, and perhaps the toughest, section of PA's rocks, run into Wind Gap for some homemade ice cream at Sweet Nanny's. About a mile east as the AT crosses PA 33.

- **Zoe's Ice Cream Emporium (Delaware Water Gap, PA).** Another stop for a frozen treat directly on the Trail, just as you leave PA. The décor so perfectly recreates the feel of an old fashion ice cream shoppe ... ice cream sodas, malts, grand sundaes and banana splits ... you'll think you've traveled through time.

- **Bellvale Farms Creamery (Bellvale, NY).** There is no 0.2 walk off the Trail that we recommend more than this brief trip to the Trail's best ice cream. Take in the extraordinary view south towards High Point, NJ from the creamery's site on the top of Peter Mountain.

- **Heaven Hill Farm (Vernon, NJ).** Another convenient (just 0.1W) and hiker-friendly stop where you can indulge in local, homemade ice cream (and fresh produce) before climbing up Wawayanda Mountain to the Pinwheel vista.

- **Diane's Twist (Cheshire, MA).** Soft-serve as well as hand-scooped ice cream, plus milkshakes and great meatball subs (and other sandwiches), right on the Trail in the center of town. Grab a cone for now and a sub for later, as you make your way up Mt. Greylock.

- **Green Mountain Hostel (Manchester Center, VT).** With Ben & Jerry pints being sold for $1 (yes, $1) we had to give a shout out for this exceptional opportunity, very few can pass up.

- **Cloudland Farm Market (Woodstock, VT).** A short (0.3W) walk to a local, farm store with produce, cheese, and homemade ice cream.

- **Moose Scoops (Warren, NH).** Always on NH's "best" list, serving local (Hatchland Farms) soft-serve and Gifford's of Maine's hard, hand-scooped ice cream. This great stop is 3.4 miles east, but a simple visit if staying at Hiker's Welcome in Glencliff.

- **Morano Gelato (Hanover, NH).** Like most things in Hanover, platinum in quality but also in price. Morano spoons small dishes of real gelato in a variety of exquisite flavors –Enjoying this gourmet treat, you'll almost think you're in Italy. Almost…

- **Caratunk House (Caratunk, ME).** Paul doesn't offer the typical frozen treat, but a Platinum-Blazer welcomes milkshakes in the ice cream category… especially when there are essentially no other ingredients. Even if you don't stay, indulge in the shake at Caratunk House.

- **Abol Bridge Camp Store. (Just south of AT entrance to Baxter State Park.)** It's just a window to the outside, but it sells Maine's own Gifford ice cream – an exceptional treat to snack on as you gaze upon Katahdin up close from the bridge.

- **Appalachian Trail Café (Millinocket, ME).** What better way to celebrate reaching your destination at the top of Katahdin then at the iconic thru-hiker themed café. We dare you to indulge in the Summit Sundae Challenge.

| **Best Platinum Ice Cream/Milkshake:** |
| Bellvale Farms Creamery |
| (Bellvale, NY) |

You may have your own favorite ice cream locale from your youth, but we challenge you to put those memories up against Bellvale Farms. Even for non-hikers, this farm's frozen treat is something for the record books and worthy of any vacationer's stop. Just an easy 0.2W off the AT in southern New York, every hiker we spoke with agreed this is a must-visit site on anyone's thru-hike. Not only are the ice cream and milkshakes remarkable, but it sits atop Mt. Peter with exceptional views of the valley west ... a perfect setting for a perfect treat.

In addition, Bellvale Farms is very hiker friendly. The owners provide an outdoor AT "hiker center" where they offer a spigot to refill water, and outlets to recharge electronic devices. In addition, on your way to the Creamery is Hot Dog Plus, a great little hot dog stand with a $5.50 lunch special: 2 dogs, chips and a canned drink. Double-dip this off-trail meal with a Bellvale Farms ice cream ... you can't find an off-trail experience much better than that!

Runners-Up:
- Caratunk House (Caratunk, ME)
- Waysides in Shenandoah National Park

Honorable Mention:
- Zoe's Ice Cream Emporium (Delaware Water Gap, PA)

RTK doing the "Half-Gallon Challenge"

Bellvale Farms

Platinum Breweries & Pubs

It's no secret that thru-hikers appreciate the opportunity to enjoy a beer when they have a chance to get off-trail. Sharkbait and RTK confess to seeking out this diversion from time to time (read: as often as possible). Fortunately, with the increasingly popularity of craft beer producers, more and more interesting locales to enjoy an IPA or lager are available each year. The Appalachian Trail community is not foreign to this movement, and is home to quite a few special brewery experiences, large and small. Some even have tasting rooms, restaurants, and hiker amenities attached. RTK recalls his favorite pub visit:

> *I was working my way through Vermont in and out of a gang that would number nine by the time we all reached New Hampshire. After enjoying an incredible sunset atop Killington, we descended to the base to gather together again that night at McGrath's at the Inn at the Long Trail. We happened to visit on a night of live music. The smelly hikers hung in the back, but that didn't prevent wonderful service of Celtic specialties as pints of Guinness and Smithwick's flowed. We stayed for the last encore and closed the bar down as we bought drinks for the band. For Bearfoot, Lil Blue, Gizmo, Mrs. T, Savage, Po and me, it was likely one of the most memorable of off trail evenings. (The group followed this evening with back-to-back 19-mile slackpacks and then headed into the Hanover to rest before the Whites.)*

Some locations in this section are just a good old-fashioned place to drink a beer, others are all-around brewery experiences with tours and more. Of all the chapters in this book, we expect this to evolve the most from year to year.

Listing of Platinum Breweries & Pubs on the Appalachian Trail:

- **Bacchus Beer & Growlers (Hiawassee, GA).** With 15 rotating and seasonal taps to choose from, there is something for everyone at this stop on the shores of Lake Chatuge. Fun fact, this bar is named for the Roman god of the grape harvest, winemaking, frivolity and unrestrained partying.

- **Lazy Hiker Brewing Co. (Franklin, NC).** They don't have a full kitchen, but a food truck typically sits outside in the parking lot. Great beer and a great place to spend the day while taking a (likely much needed) zero day in Franklin.

- **Rock House Lodge (inside Outdoor 76 at Franklin, NC).** Yes, there is a craft brewery in the back section of this infamous trail outfitter. Every thru-hiker will appreciate a stop here, whether for the expert boot fitting advice, the free bandana … or a pint of their 18 season beers on tap.

- **Spring Creek Tavern (Hot Springs, NC).** Considered by many to be the "best trail town", Hot Springs has their share of greats for every Platinum-Blaze category. When it comes to pubs, that vote easily goes here. Great beer on tap, excellent food, and outdoor seating overlooking Spring Creek.

- **Smoky Mountain Brewery (Gatlinburg, TN).** Gatlinburg is one of those towns you love to hate and hate to love. It's a great place for a break from the mountains, but also a gigantic tourist trap. Instead of buying the gimmicky moonshine in town, stop here for a real drink to go with typical pub fare.

- **The Station at 19E (Roan Mountain, TN).** Host to a new 27-bed bunkhouse, the Station at 19E makes a great stop greater. This onsite craft beer pub provides excellent live music, karaoke, or just a place to unwind with a pint. And if you can play the stage, you may be able to negotiate a free bed for the night (Ripple in 2018 did).

- **Damascus Brewery (Damascus, VA).** With seasonal options like Beaver Fever Porter, Bimbo Blonde, and Honey Mango Sour ... this brewery is one of the more eclectic options on the list. But with limited beer proprietors in Damascus, you'll likely make your way here regardless of what is on tap.

- **Devil's Backbone (Roseland, VA).** Built in the likeness of a Swiss Alps brewpub, Devil's Backbone is a beer drinker haven in the Blue Ridge Mountains. One visit, and you'll know why they call themselves the "Music, Food, Camping, & Beer Wonderland."

- **Front Royal Brewing Co. (Front Royal, VA).** Nestled in the beautiful Shenandoah Valley, you'll find this brewery just down the street from PaveMint BBQ (another great Front Royal stop). In their words, "Craft beer mecca, gourmet restaurant, sports bar, beer hall, dope outdoor area – take your pick. FRB has it all."

- **Jacob's Restaurant (Dalton, MA).** With a "neighborhood bar" atmosphere, you'll feel right at home walking in to Jacob's for a beer. Around the corner from the Shamrock Village, and quite a few steps up from Paddy's on Main.

- **Madison Brewing Company (Bennington, VT).** A family business in downtown Bennington, the Madisons provide a warm and inviting atmosphere in their large downstairs and upstairs dining rooms. The full restaurant and bar menu will have whatever your heart desires, and the variety of beers they can weekly won't disappoint.

- **Hop 'n Moose Brewery (Rutland, VT).** Locally sourced food pairs well with the hand-crafted ales and lagers in this downtown Rutland brewery. It's worth a stop, but honestly, it's just really fun to say its name. "Hey, which way to the Hop 'n Moose!?"

- **McGrath's Irish Pub (Rutland, VT).** After descending from Killington Mountain, head straight to McGrath's at The Inn at the Long Trail. Old routes of the AT take you right to McGrath's front door where you can get a property poured Guinness Stout. With true Celtic influence, consider some Irish stew or Shepard's Pie while you enjoy the live music (weekends).

- **Norwich Inn, Alehouse & Brewery (Norwich, VT).** One of the top breweries in Vermont and the home of Jasper Murdock Ale. Large in stature but small in space, the Norwich Inn is a great appetizer to the luxuries of Hanover that await across the river.

- **Woodstock Inn Station & Brewery (North Woodstock, NH).** Grab a drink, take a tour, eat in, dine out, or stay at the inn … there is much to be enjoyed at this special New Hampshire brewery. Try the new Frosty Goggles après ski pale ale that "pairs nicely with your feet up, boots off."

- **One Love Brewery (Lincoln, NH).** If you take a zero day before entering the White Mountains, add this taproom to your stop list. As you unwind in this vacation resort town, Master Brewer Michael Snyder will treat you to one of his many award-winning craft beers within this charming renovated paper mill along Main St.

- **Sarge's Sports Pub & Grub (Rangeley, ME).** One of the better sports bars along the Trail, and for good reason. Rangeley is home to quite a few summer vacationers, that frequent this Maine locale for the excellent choice of beer, burgers, wings and more.

- **Kennebec River Brewery (Caratunk, ME).** It has to be mentioned, but we may advise against a visit. This restaurant and brewery, managed by the Northern Outdoors outdoor adventure company, will likely be overrun by white-water rafting groups and families. The food and beer are nice, but by this point in your thru-hike, you'll likely want to avoid this crowd.

Best Platinum Brewery & Pub:

Devil's Backbone
(Roseland, VA)

Nestled at the base of the Blue Ridge Mountains, this brewpub has it all. Both RTK and Sharkbait made it a point to stop here (and actually, RTK did on all his prep-hikes as well), and although not directly on the Trail, a visit is well worth the extra effort.

With nearly 50 beers on tap, Devil's Backbone has been serving up quality craft brews for years from Steve and Heidi Crandalls. The vision for this brewpub came after a ski trip to the Alps, where the Crandalls dreamed to create a European-style brewery for hikers and skiers to drink and tell stories of their adventures. And although purchased by Anheuser-Busch in 2016, it still maintains the same charm and award-winning beer today that it always has.

While visiting Devil's Backbone, you'll also enjoy restaurant fare from the delicious oak wood-fired kitchen, an elegant outdoor space worthy of a beautiful outdoor mountain wedding, a distillery of whiskey spirits, a cigar lounge, outdoor fire pits, campsites, showers and more. And, for a true Platinum-Blaze experience, you can even rent a private luxury home on property.

Runners-Up:
- McGrath's Irish Pub (Rutland, VA)
- Lazy Hiker Brewing Co. – Franklin, NC

Honorable Mention:
- Woodstock Inn Station & Brewery (North Woodstock, NH)
- Spring Creek Tavern (Hot Springs, NC)

Platinum Delis

Although we've written that "there is perhaps no food more sought after by thru-hikers than pizza, burgers and ice cream," the delicatessen holds a very special place in the heart of most thru-hikers – especially for those northbounders who finally make it to New York and New England. For those unfamiliar, these roadside convenience stores and marketplaces are casual places to grab a fresh-made sandwich and snack. The delicacy these provide cannot be undersold, as the only real comparison along the Trail in the South is possible Subway restaurant or pre-made grocery store selection. Being able to not carry lunch for multiple days, while also having a fresh sandwich with fresh meat and bread, is a great treat that this section of the AT offers. Here is one of Sharkbait's recommended deli stops.

Some delis require a short half-mile or less walk off the trail for a treat, but one special place is directly on the white-blazed path. After crossing the Hudson River near Fort Montgomery and battling the tourists day-hiking up Anthony's Nose, I was rewarded with the Appalachian Market in Garrison, NY. Although just a roadside pitstop along NY Route 9, it was lunch and dinner for the rest of my day. Sure, they are well-stocked in typical hiker supplies, but I quickly walked passed the ramen noodles and granola bars and stepped up to the deli counter. I quickly engulfed a huge chicken cutlet sandwich outside on the picnic table, indulged in an Italian Ice for dessert, and then ordered a Boars Head turkey and cheese hoagie to go for my dinner.

There are some options in the South, though Spartan in comparison until you hit the Northeast. In fact, it's often said that when you hit New York and New Jersey, you can stop at a deli every day for weeks. It takes a bit of planning and coordination, but this "deli-blazing" is very possible for the steadfast hiker to achieve, and highly recommended for the Platinum-Blazer.

Listing of Platinum Delis on the Appalachian Trail:

- Frogtown Market (Franklin, NC)
- Lazy Hiker Brewing Co. (Franklin, NC)
- Amish Cupboard (Buena Vista, VA)
- Green Mountain Store – (south of Boiling Springs, PA)
- Village Farmer & Bakery (Delaware Water Gap, PA)
- Yellow Cottage Deli & Bakery (Branchville, NJ)
- Vinny's Deli (Pawling, NY)
- Horler's Store (Unionville, NY)
- Tony's Deli (Pawling, NY)
- Appalachian Market (Garrison, NY)
- Ben's Deli (Wingdale, NY)
- Cornwall Country Market (Cornwall Bridge, CT)
- LaBonne's Market (Salisbury, CT)
- Mountaintop Market Deli (5.0N of RPH Shelter, Stormville, NY)
- Panini Café (Kent, CT)
- Toymaker's Café (Falls Village, CT)
- Angelina's Subs (Dalton, MA)
- Diane's Twist (Cheshire, MA)
- Egremont Market (South Egremont, MA)
- Dalton General Store (Dalton, MA)
- Bromley Market & Deli (Bromley Mountain Resort - Peru, VT)
- Nichols Store & Deli (Danby, VT)
- Yellow Deli (Rutland, VT)
- Loretta's Deli (Clarendon, VT)
- Zoey's Deli (Manchester Center, VT)
- Dan & Whitt's General Store (Norwich, VT)
- Lyme Country Store (Lyme, NH)
- Merland's Deli (North Woodstock, NH)
- Wayne's Market (Lincoln, NH)
- Etna General Store (Etna, NH)
- Andover General Store (Andover, ME)
- Fotter's Store (Stratton, ME)
- Monson General Store (Monson, ME)

Best Platinum Deli:

Horler's Store
(Unionville, NY)

Many hikers will have their own favorite deli once past the Mason Dixon Line, but we believe Horler's Store deserves special recognition. None could be a Best Platinum Deli without fresh rolls, excellent meats, a broad selection, and pleasant service ... and Horler's serves all of that, along with some deliciously tempting baked treats.

Horler's also helps define the epitome of "hiker friendly." Not only do they provide a lovingly long New England front porch, but they equip it with charging stations for hikers. Every patron that passes by seems to understand the AT, often stopping to chat with hikers with genuine interest and helpful suggestions. (Specifically, that one could retro-blaze down Main Street, where the AT previously passed. RTK and a number of fellow thru-hikers found it hard to head back to the Trail because the food and welcoming environment were so delightful, comfortable and inviting. As one fellow hiker shared with us," be very careful of the red chairs in the front of the building here if you're passing through town. They will trap you forever if you try to sit in them and you will never leave Unionville."

Thru-hikers working their way to New Jersey need to recall that Unionville is actually in New York, but a planned stop at Horler's is before the AT reaches the AT's 9th state. Horler's also helps to manage the town's free camping ground across the street from the store and next to the US post office. Yes, if you're thinking, "if I camp near Horler's, I can double-dip this platinum stop," you are spot on!

Runners-Up:
- Zoey's Deli (Manchester Center, VT)
- Fotter's Store (Stratton, ME)

Honorable Mention:
- Monson General Store (Monson, ME) – Great place to pack a lunch/dinner before the 100-Mile Wilderness.

Special Consideration:
- There are some good delis in the southern Appalachian Mountains, but their frequency and availability is too sparse or sporadic to "deli-blaze." However, once a northbound thru-hiker passes into NJ, opportunities abound to practice that art form. Check out the suggested Deli-Blaze Itinerary in the Appendix.

Horler's General Store – Uniontown, NY

Platinum Burgers

Burgers and Pizza ... the crème de la crème of hiker cravings. The places identified below represent the best recommendations to curb those frequent cravings for a good hamburger or cheeseburger on the Trail. As we did in the restaurant category, we used proximity and ease of access to the Trail to define our choices. For this reason, you'll see great burger places like The Vault in Ashville, NC and Texas Tavern in Roanoke, VA excluded. However, we did include the Appalachian Trail Café despite its distance from the Trail because it is visited so often by thru-hikers post-summit ... and bears the right name.

Listing of Platinum Burgers on the Appalachian Trail:

- Copeland's Burgers & Southern Eats (Blairsville, GA)
- Big Daddy's (Helen, GA)
- Sundance Grill (Hiawassee, GA)
- Lazy Hiker Brewery (Franklin, NC)
- Motor Grill (Franklin, NC)
- River's End (Nantahala Outdoor Center, NC)
- Spring Creek Tavern (Hot Springs, NC)
- Smokey Mountain Diner (Hot Springs, NC)
- Smokey Mountain Brewery (Gatlinburg, TN)
- Spelunker's (Front Royal, VA)
- Brushy Mountain Outpost (Bland, VA)
- Barn (Atkins, VA)
- Tailgate Grill (Waynesboro, VA)
- Jake's Bar & Grill (Waynesboro, VA)
- Waysides (Shenandoah National Park, VA)
- Potomac Grill (Harpers Ferry, WV)
- Timbers (Fayetteville, PA)
- Pine Grove Furnace General Store (PGFSP, PA)
- The Doyle Hotel (Duncannon, PA)
- Tony's Deli (Pawling, NY)
- Big W's Roadside BBQ (Wingdale, PA)
- J.P. Gifford (Kent, CT)

- Kingsley Tavern (Kent, CT)
- Toymaker's Café (Falls Village, CT)
- Jacob's Pub (Dalton, MA)
- Gypsy Joint (Great Barrington, MA)
- 20 Railroad Pub House (Great Barrington, MA)
- Water Street Grill (Williamstown, MA)
- Zoey's Double Hex (Manchester Center, VT)
- Table 24 (Rutland, VT)
- Molly's (Hanover, NH)
- Murphy's on the Green (Hanover, NH)
- Black Mountain Burger (Lincoln, NH)
- Libby's Bistro & SAalt Pub (Gorham, NH)
- Sarge's Sports Pub & Grub (Rangeley, ME)
- Bag & Kettle Restaurant (Carrabassett Valley, ME)
- White House Landing (100-Mile Wilderness, ME)
- White Wolf Inn (Stratton, ME)
- Appalachian Trail Café (Millinocket, ME)

Best Platinum Burger:
The Doyle Hotel
(Duncannon, PA)

It would be difficult to find any aspiring AT thru-hiker that is unfamiliar with The Doyle Hotel. Reaching this community landmark in Duncannon, is a pivotal moment in one's journey. This historic lodge dates originally from the 1770s and has become an institution among Appalachian Trail hikers … even if its accommodations are among the worst one can find. Yes, there is a reason this hotel is not found anywhere else in this guide. Charles Dickens may have famously stayed here once, but simply put, spending a night at The Doyle today is as far from platinum as we can imagine.

However, the restaurant and bar are another story, which is why The Doyle tops our list for Best Platinum Burger. Partially because it's directly on the AT path, partially because it's a fond memory of Pennsylvania (before the rocks), but also because the burger and fries truly are just that good. Always fresh, never frozen, the patties are a greasy delight of calories that rivals the best patty you've ever cooked on your grill back home. Drop your pack outside the restaurant, take a seat at the bar, chat with the owners Pat and Vicky and enjoy the best The Doyle has to offer, accompanied by a variety of cold drafts from nearby Yuengling (the nation's oldest brewery).

Runners-Up:
- White House Landing (100-Mile Wilderness, ME)
- White Wolf Inn (Stratton, ME)
- Sarge's Sports Pub & Grub (Rangeley, ME)
- Gypsy Joint (Great Barrington, MA)
- Copeland's Burgers & Southern Eats (Blairsville, GA)

Yes, a lobster roll (with steamer clams)!

Platinum Pizza

No, this isn't an argument between Chicago deep dish or a New York slice. In fact, you'll be hard pressed to find anything resembling Geno's East or Joe's Pizza in the Appalachian Mountains. And if you just cringed at us listing Geno's over Giordano's, or Joe's over Grimaldi's Pizza ... you'll understand how tough this category is to rate.[3]

We, like most every other thru-hiker, LOVE pizza. There is just something about visions of fluffy dough and gooey cheese that inexplicably force feet to walk to town. Although we recognize that pizza is rarely a platinum level treat, we too craved it so heavily that we realized a list of Platinum Pizza locations was needed. (Even if some of our best recommendations here are just frozen pies made in convenience store ovens). RTK's favorite pizza story demonstrates just how much love and determination for this simple Italian fare can be found on the AT.

Locals, ridge-runners and fellow thru-hikers all encouraged us not to miss Timbers Restaurant. Irish Paul, Phin (his mate from the Emerald Island), and I showed up at Timbers' door, yet it was closed for Memorial Day. Argh! We checked into Trail of Hope hostel, a little further down the road, to try to recover from this setback. Undaunted, Irish Paul borrowed the hostel's bicycle and headed off to the ("its just .7 miles down the road") quick-stop. It was already dark and on-going road construction was obvious when Irish Paul pedaled away.

Time passed, Phin and I began to wonder where he was. Finally, around 10 p.m. Irish Paul returned with two large pizza boxes. As he pulled other snacks and beverages from his pockets and laid the boxes down, he related where he had been (which story I'll try to relate in Paul's own Irish brogue).

"Well, first, it's well mahre like 1.7 miles dan .7 miles. Den, I stroehck wance o' de prahtrudin manhahle

---

[3] A native of Connecticut born in New Haven, RTK argues that Sally's or Pepe's would beat out anything from Chicago or NYC.

96

cahvers (translation: *I struck one of the protruding manhole covers*), and crashed de bike. De chain came ahff, so I 'ad to fex dat. When I finally 'ad de pezzas made and started back I realized I cooehldn't ride safely and keep de pezza flat and oehpright, so I toehcked dem oehnder me arm and rahde back."

It's a harrowing story, even without the Celtic accent. As we opened the boxes, we saw that the difficult journey had transformed the "Everything Supreme" pizzas into calzones as the cooked dough and toppings had slid to the bottom of the box when Irish Paul held them upright under his arm during the return trip. The only other hostel guest and the caretaker joined us for a fun night that proved to be my latest night during the entire hike as we didn't retire until after midnight.

As you can see, platinum pizza is not always based on ingredients, style, or even taste ... the best pizzas are the one nearest the Trail when you want it most. (Or even better, the ones that deliver right to you at a shelter!). We hope you have the determination of Irish Paul to seek out this favorite dish at some of these stops along the Trail.

Listing of Platinum Pizza on the Appalachian Trail:

- Mountain Crossings (frozen, but so welcome!)
- Big Al's Pizza (Hiawassee, GA)
- Standing Bear hostel (after just leaving the Smokies, like arriving at Mountain Crossings, this frozen pizza can be excellent)
- Primo's Italian (Erwin, TN)
- Rocky's Pizza (Erwin, TN)
- Damascus Pizza Co. Bar & Grill (Damascus, VA)
- Pizza Perfect (Marion, VA and delivers to Partnership Shelter)
- Lentini's (Daleville, VA) (worth the 1.0N of Three Lil Pigs)

- Bear's Den (Northern Virginia) (another frozen pie, but combine it with a pint of Ben & Jerry's, a cold drink, and a bunk and you have one of the Trail's get values)
- Mena's Pizzeria (Harper's Ferry, WV)
- Vince's Pizza (Smithsburg, MD)
- Rutter's Convenience Store (Fayetteville, PA) (a/k/a "Irish Paul's C-Store")
- Do's Pizza (Pine Grove, PA) (delivers to 501 Shelter)
- Anile's Ristorante & Pizzeria (Boiling Springs, PA)
- Doughboys of the Poconos (Delaware Water Gap, PA)
- Bear Mountain Pizza (Highland Falls, NY)
- Gaudino's Pizza & Pasta (Pawling, NY)
- Village Pizza (Pawling, NY)
- Kent Pizza Garden (Kent, CT)
- Baba Louie's (Great Barrington, MA)
- Olympic Pizza (Williamstown, MA)
- Sam's Wood Fired Pizza (Manchester Center, VT)
- Hop 'n Moose Brewing (Rutland, VT)
- Ramunto's Brick & Brew Pizzeria (Hanover, NH) (free slice for thru-hikers)
- Mr. Pizza (Gorham, NH) (much better than its name)
- GH Pizza (Lincoln, NH)
- La Vista Italian (Lincoln, NH)
- Lakeshore House (Monson, ME)
- A.E. Robinson Convenience Store (Monson, ME)
- Angelo's Pizza Grille (Millinocket, ME)

If Irish Paul's determination was not enough to convince you yet of the thru-hiker's craving for a "slice," consider "Rocky's Pizza Challenge" – an AT tradition we picked up from some of our fellow thru-hikers. This challenge involves running south on the Trail from the Curly Maple shelter just north of the trailhead in Erwin, TN, which is 4.3 miles, hitching a ride to Rocky's Pizza (another 5+ miles), and returning to the shelter with several large pizzas and at least a case of beer. (Yes, we verified the veracity of this "tradition".). Now that we have your attention, lets see who was selected for the Best Platinum Pizza.

Best Platinum Pizza:

Anile's Ristorante & Pizzeria
(Boiling Springs, PA)

In truth, you could put Anile's in the best restaurant category, since their salads, subs, and pastas are also outstanding. But the real treat of this family-owned restaurant is the pizza. Anile and his son setup shop just a couple hundred feet down the road from the Appalachian Trail Conservancy office in Boiling Springs, where they have created a restaurant that should be on every hiker's must-stop list when they get to town.

Although Sharkbait is a sucker for a good old-fashioned cheese pizza, even he had to admit the specialty pies made up here are worthy of a hiker dinner (and breakfast/lunch the next day, because food preservation and refrigeration standards have no place on the AT). Whether you choose the Eggplant Parmigiana, BBQ Chicken, or Meat Lovers Pizza, you'll enjoy one of the Trail's best offerings after a long day of pasture-land walking.

Runners-Up:
- Mr. Pizza (Gorham, NH)
- Angelo's Pizza Grille (Millinocket, ME)

Honorable Mention:
- Mountain Crossings (Blairsville, GA) – yes it is just frozen pizza, but it's the first hot food option after 4+ days hiking NOBO.

Platinum Value Restaurants

Thru-hikers have many favorite restaurants along the Appalachian Trail, most of which are far from places of fine dining. Yet, they are conveniently located, hiker-friendly options offering all-you-can-eat or low prices within most thru-hikers limited budget. In a sense, they are "value" restaurants.

While we do not mean to be unkind to any of these establishments (in fact, we love these places too), this is a guide to Platinum-Blazing and therefore they don't quite fit in with the other fine dining establishments. However, while we love visiting these places and find the meals great, in reality, this greatness is relative to people spending lengthy time in the woods. For example, RTK ate at and thoroughly enjoyed La Barranca, the Mexican restaurant in Pearisburg, VA. And although locals told RTK it was one of the town's best restaurants, it was still just basic Mexican food you can get anywhere – excellent basic Mexican food, but nothing extraordinary ... nothing *platinum*. With those remarks in mind, here is our list of what we found to be thru-hiker's Platinum Value Restaurants.

Listing of Platinum Value Restaurants on the Appalachian Trail:

- Daniel's Steakhouse (Hiawassee, GA)
- Lazy Hiker Brewing Co. (Franklin, NC)
- Smokey Mountain Diner (Hot Springs, NC)
- Highlander BBQ (Roan Mountain, TN)
- Bob's Dairyland (Roan Mountain, TN)
- La Barranca (Pearisburg, VA)
- The Homeplace (Catawba, VA)
- Three Little Pigs (Daleville, VA)
- Ming Garden (Waynesboro, VA)
- Timbers Restaurant (Fayetteville, PA)
- Pine Grove Furnace General Store (PGFSP, PA)
- Gyp's Tavern (Branchville, NJ)
- Panini Café (Kent, CT)
- Jacob's Pub (Dalton, MA)

- Inn at Long Trail (Rutland, VT)
- Yellow Deli (Rutland, VT)
- Cilantro Taco (Manchester Center, VT)
- Little Red Hen (Andover, ME)
- Kennebec River Brewery/Northern Outdoors (Caratunk, ME)
- Spring Creek BBQ (Monson, ME)
- White House Landing (100-Mile Wilderness, ME)

Best Platinum Value Restaurant:

The Homeplace
(Catawba, VA)

One of the most popular visits anywhere on the Appalachian Trail is enjoying dinner at The Homeplace. Hikers typically stop here (and return here) when traversing the Triple Crown of Virginia – Dragon's Tooth, McAfee's Knob, and Tinker Cliffs. In fact, RTK's friend Mighty Blue shared in his popular AT hiker podcast that during his 2014 thru-hike he stayed at Four Pines Hostel three consecutive nights while hiking through the area, just so he could have dinner each night at The Homeplace.

For us here at the Platinum-Blaze, a stop at The Homeplace tops this category even though it didn't quite make the Platinum Restaurant section. A meal at The Homeplace isn't fine dining like a meal at Caffé Rel, but there may not be any stop along the Trail more revered. We are delighted to recognize the uniqueness and enjoyment of a visit here

RTK stopped in for dinner after finishing a day-hike of Dragon's Tooth from the Nidday Shelter with a former law partner and reported his experience like this:

We thoroughly enjoyed the standard, family-style, AYCE, fixed price meal, which consists of pulled pork (Thursdays only), roast beef, country ham, fried chicken, mashed

potatoes, green beans, Cole slaw, pinto beans, and fruit cobbler with ice cream for dessert. But to focus solely on the food would miss the wonderful service and hiker-friendly atmosphere. Not surprisingly, while I enjoyed my meal and time at The Homeplace, I ran into not fewer than twenty fellow-hikers, a dozen of whom I knew and with whom I had spent time hiking.

As so many before us have said, it's simply a stop along the Trail that no thru-hiker should miss.

Runner-Up:
- Ming Garden (Waynesboro, VA)

Honorable Mention:
- Little Red Hen (Andover, ME)

Chapter 9

PLATINUM OFF-TRAIL SITES, VISITS & SPECIAL EXPERIENCES

The Appalachian Trail provides many opportunities for thru-hikers to enjoy the finer things in life along its 2,200-mile path (yes, there is more to a luxury hike than just lodging and food). In this chapter, we divide these opportunities into four extraordinary categories for Platinum-Blazers to consider, which we believe will elevate their overall hike experience along the way. These are the luxuries of the mind, the spirit, and the will to hike on ... a short blue-blaze trail to an epic waterfall, a bus ride to a vibrant city, or an excursion to a historic site, and more.

Because of the importance of motivation and mentality along a thru-hike, these platinum experiences cannot be undersold. Because of this, this chapter is dedicated to the sites, visits, and special locations we believe are platinum among all others. This includes:

- **Waterfalls, Vistas & Other Blue Blaze Opportunities**. Points of interest for thru-hikers that are off the official AT, but still in nature. Of the countless side trips that crisscross the white-blazed Appalachian Trail, these various blue-blaze trail experiences will take you to many of the best views and serene moments in nature.

- **Special AT Experiences.** Some places don't fit in a category, and are just so unique and special to the Appalachian Trail, they demand a section of their own. Taking in these moments will contribute to an extraordinary, truly platinum, AT experience.

- **Trail Towns.** Similarly, but more focused on the communities that are more directly involved with thru-hikers, we provide Platinum-Blaze evaluation on the very best Trail Towns to pass through, stay at, and indulge in.

- **City Visits & Unique Side Trips**. Albeit further than 1 mile away, the AT provides access to some great American cities that hikers new to the region will typically want to visit (e.g. Washington DC, Boston, New York). In addition, there are many unique and remote side trips within a comfortable distance as well, such as Gettysburg Battlefield or the Yuengling Brewery. These are all worth consideration for a couple zero days.

No thru-hiker could ever see or visit every location in this chapter, but by knowing which are worth the effort in advance, we hope future hikers can plan their trip around the ones they can, and make an already incredible journey more platinum in style.

Platinum Waterfalls, Vistas & Other Blue-Blaze Opportunities

In this section, we identify the best blue-blaze experiences that offer great natural features one should consider taking some time to visit. Be it waterfalls, summits, beaches, or other, we believe these features (like Thoreau Falls or Old Speck summit) are so magnificent that even with the additional (minimal) hiking, the side trip is worth it.

One of the reasons to spend 6 months doing a thru-hike of the AT is to enjoy the physical beauty from Georgia to Maine, and although some take extra consideration, many are already the inspiration for a person's thru-hike.

Fortunately, some of the best views take no extra time or effort to see at all, as they lie directly on the Appalachian Trail's footpath. Since we know every hiker will certainly see these points of interest directly, we did not include them in our blue-blaze list opportunities. However, we strongly encourage every hiker to take in these moments with as much time as they can afford, since there are few experiences more anticipated and beautiful on the Trail than these.

1. The Pinnacle, Pennsylvania
2. Clingmans Dome, Tennessee
3. McAfee Knob, Virginia
4. Tinker Cliffs, Virginia
5. Dragon's Tooth, Virginia
6. Max Patch, North Carolina
7. Grayson Highlands, Virginia
8. Mount Moosilauke, New Hampshire
9. Mount Washington, New Hampshire
10. Baldpate, Maine

Although these represent the commonly agreed-upon "best" views on the Trail, there are other great summits and vistas, such as Saddleback Mountain (ME) or Blood Mountain (GA), that also require no additional steps off the white-blazed path. We encourage you to enjoy each of these you come upon, whether named in guidebooks or not, while on your journey. These are moments that make the miles of ups and downs worth it.

However, not every great view is right in front of you, and some take a bit of extra walking to see. Hikers would never consider taking every blue-blaze experience they come across, but we believe these should take special consideration and inclusion.

Listing of Platinum Waterfalls, Vistas, and Blue-Blaze Opportunities:

- Amicalola Falls (Approach Trail) – S of Springer Mtn summit
- Long Creek Falls (Mile 5) [0.1W]
- Standing Indian Mountain summit (Mile 87) [0.2E]
- Siler Bald summit (Mile 113) [0.2W]
- Shuckstack Fire Tower (Mile 170) [0.1E]
- Charlies Bunion (Mile 211) [0.1W]
- Mt. Cammerer (Mile 235) [0.6W]
- Blackstack Cliffs (Mile 298) [0.1W]
- Roan High Bluff/old Cloudland Hotel site (Mile 378) [0.1E]
- Rhododendron Gardens (Mile 378) [0.5E]
- Grassy Ridge (Mile 382) [0.5E]

- Jones Falls (Mile 400) [0.1E]
- Coon Den Falls (Mile 418) [0.8E]
- Watauga Dam Visitor Center (Mile 418) [0.5E]
- Mount Rogers summit (Mile 498) [0.5W] - Highest point in Virginia
- Settlers Museum (Mile 542) [0.1E]
- Dismal Falls (Mile 611) [0.3W]
- Apple Orchard Falls (Mile 768) [1.1W]
- Spy Rock (Mile 824) [0.1E]
- Humpback Rocks (Mile 852) [0.3W]
- Glass Hollow overlook (Mile 856) [0.2E]
- Lewis Falls (Mile 924) [0.5W]
- Stony Man summit (Mile 934). [0.2W] – Highest point in Shenandoah National Park
- Jewell Hollow overlook (Mile 938) [0.1E]
- ATC Headquarters (Mile 1024) [0.2W]
- Maryland Heights (Mile 1025) [1.7W] – Views to Harper's Ferry
- Weaverton Cliffs (Mile 1029) [0.05E]
- Washington Monument (Mile 1044) [0.1W]
- Annapolis Rocks (Mile 1049) [0.2W]
- High Rock overlook (Mile 1063) [0.1E]
- Old Coal Mining settlement (Mile 1,173) [0.7W]
- Waterville Iron Bridge (Mile 1183.5)
- Hawk Mountain Sanctuary trail (Mile 1235) [2.0W] – Wild bird sanctuary
- Dunnfield Creek Falls (Mile 1296) [0.25E]
- Buttermilk Falls (Mile 1315) [1.5W]
- High Point Monument (Mile 1338) [0.3W] – Highest point in New Jersey
- Pinwheels Vista (Mile 1359) [0.1W]
- Wawayanda Mountain (Mile 1359) [0.8E]
- Anthony's Nose (Mile 1406) [0.6E] – Views to Hudson River
- Guilder Pond dam (Mile 1513) [0.1W]
- Stratton Mountain Gondola (Mile 1638) [0.8]
- White Rock Cliffs (Mile 1675) [0.25W]

- Mt. Killington summit (Mile 1695) [0.2E] – Restaurant & 360 views at summit
- The Lookout (cabin) (Mile 1719) [0.1W]
- Mt. Cube north peak (Mile 1779) [0.3W]
- Webster Slide Mountain (Mile 1790) [0.7W]
- AMC Greenleaf hut (Mile 1824) [1.1W]
- Mt. Liberty (Mile 1818) [0.2E]
- Thoreau Falls (Mile 1840) [0.2E]
- Mt. Eisenhower summit (Mile 1854) [0.3W]
- Mt. Monroe summit (Mile 1856) [0.3W]
- Mt. Clay summit (Mile 1859) [0.1E]
- Mt. Jefferson summit (Mile 1860) [0.3W]
- AMC Carter Notch hut (Mile 1877) [0.2E]
- Moriah summit (Mile 1887) [0.2W]
- Old Speck Mountain summit (Mile 1920) [0.3E]
- Spaulding Mountain summit (Mile 1990) [0.1E]
- Historic bronze plaque (Mile 1991) – marks date/place of completion of AT
- Sugarloaf Mountain summit (Mile 1992) [0.6E]
- Gulf Hagas (Mile 2108) (5.2-mile loop trail) – The "Grand Canyon of the East"
- Katahdin view from Rainbow Lake (Mile 2163) [0.1W]
- Knife Edge trail (Mile 2190.9) – trail down from Mt. Katahdin to Pamola Peak

Best Platinum Waterfalls, Vistas & Other Blue-Blaze Opportunities

Neither Sharkbait nor RTK took every blue-blaze to these sites, but we visited many, and think all are worth the effort. To help prioritize what is right for future hikers, we offer some recommendations to help decide which ones are most worthy of the time. Each of these of course assumes good weather as well. However, when planning your side trips, also keep in mind that bad weather could literally erase any view from atop a recommended summit. Flexibility and adaptability are key to any thru-hike, and unfortunately you may reach Clingmans Dome on one of its 320 cloudy days per year.

- **0.1 miles or less**: Take them all! Special consideration: Jones Falls. (TN) and Charlies Bunion. (TN).

- **0.1 to 0.3 miles:** Take them as often as you can, time and weather permitting. Special consideration: Siler Bald summit (NC); White Rock Cliffs (VT); Killington summit (VT); Thoreau Falls (NH); Old Speck summit (ME).

- **0.3 to 1.0 miles:** Take what appeals to you most, but don't let the day's weariness convince you to throw out an anticipated plan. Special consideration: Mt. Cammerer or almost any of the "loop" trails to the Presidential summits not directly on the Trail.

- **1.0 miles or more:** Take what you can, being realistic of each day's miles. Special consideration: Knife Edge at Mt. Katahdin; Gulf Hagas (100-mile wilderness in Maine).

It is unrealistic to think you can do everything, and very common to let a sign-post reading 0.3M to discourage you after 100 days of hiking. But we believe these experiences are worth the extra effort and will-power to enjoy. On a clear and sunny day, you'll be happy you took the extra 1-mile round-trip visit to a private lake for a swim, or a special summit for a snack.

Platinum Special AT Experiences

Did you know you can camp at a real alpaca farm? Or help with beekeeping activities at an apiary? Who would have thought that the oldest jazz club in continuous operation in the United States or an evening of Irish music would be available on the AT? Or how about a visit to a maple farm or one of the country's oldest breweries? All this is possible and more on the AT!

Although many think of the Appalachian Trail as a wilderness experience, it actually has a fairly limited view most days. Nicknamed "the green tunnel," much of the wilderness surrounding the Trail is covered during the spring and summer by a thick green canopy of leaves, making it difficult to see much of anything beyond your immediate vicinity. But, sometimes, that wilderness opens up at the summit of a mountain or the path along a winding lake/river. That is to say, when you aren't staring at your feet to avoid the countless rocks and roots trying to trip you up.

At times, you may have to go a bit out of your way to see some of the wonderful things on the AT … and there truly are a number of remarkable and extraordinary opportunities to be had. This collection represents the best of those special experiences that we believe a thru-hiker should consider working in to their Appalachian Trail journey. Not everyone will be interested in everything listed here, but any one of them will undoubtedly add to a Platinum-Blaze experience. And we think all are worth careful consideration.

Listing of Platinum Special AT Experiences:

- **Hot Springs Resort (Hot Springs, NC).** Enjoy a mineral bath whirlpool in naturally hot water sourced from local "hot springs" that gave the town its name. Indulge in one of the many fine restaurants that line the 2-block long "downtown", visit the great outfitter, or even stop in to chat with the Hikers Ridge Ministries … whose primary goal is to provide a place for weary hikers to rest legs, recharge devices, and access WiFi.

- **Elmer's Sunnybank Inn (Hot Springs, NC).** A historic inn & hostel offering a restful retreat with a library, music room and communal organic/vegetarian meals.

- **Cantarroso Farm (Erwin, TN).** This hostel located right on the Nolichucky River is also an organic farm and apiary; ask Mike to let you help with beekeeping activities.

- **Standing Bear Farm (Hartford, TN).** Love it or hate it, SBF is a unique experience where NOBO thru-hikers are welcomed after completing the Great Smokey Mountains National Park. Lodging is Spartan, the resupply stocks may be long past expiration, but it's an experience worth having. We both enjoyed a night's rest at SBF.

- **Kincora Hiking Hostel (Hampton, TN).** A stay at this hostel near Laurel Falls brings with it a chance to meet Trail legend Bob Peoples. Among other feats, Bob has done more for trail maintenance (known particularly for leading the annual "Hard Core" trail maintenance trips) than any other person.

- **Long Neck Lair (Rural Retreat, VA).** Camping (with showers and laundry) for thru-hikers just off the Trail on a working alpaca farm; work-for-stay available.

- **Appalachian Dreamer Hiker Hostel (Ceres, VA).** Spend the night (and work) at an organic farm near Atkins or Bland, VA.

- **Quarter Way Inn (Ceres, VA).** Like Cantarroso Farm, Quarter Way is a beekeeping, organic farm. It also runs on solar power, which is part of a wonderful Trail Magic story (with hikers providing the magic).

- **Woods Hole Hostel (Giles County, VA).** Historic hostel on an organic farm with animals, yoga, massage, and communal meals set in an idyllic country. We've mentioned it enough by now that we hope you plan a visit!

- **Sufi Lodge (Troutdale, VA).** Hostel and wellness center, these Sufi Lodges (better known as Dergahs, Zawiyas or Khans) are places for spiritual aspirants to gather and "spend time advancing themselves through meditative practices and prayer."

- **Devil's Backbone Brewing Company (Roseland, VA).** More than your average brew pub, offering a world-class outdoor facility with great beer and food. Devil's Backbone has adopted the Appalachian Trail as the focus of its charitable activities (employees help the Old Dominion Appalachian Trail Club in maintaining a nearby stretch of the AT) and hosts thru-hikers in new camping facilities.

- **ATC Headquarters (Harpers Ferry, WV).** A must-stop for thru-hikers, not only to officially register and take a photo at the (informal) halfway point, but to enjoy the history, library, hiker lounge, store, and conversation with the friendly staff.

- **Twelve Tribes (Lancaster, NH; Rutland, VT & Harpers Ferry, WV).** Also known as the Yellow Deli People, these donation-based hostels welcome hikers at three locations near the Trail. Work for stay is the preferred payment, where guests help with garden or animal chores at an organic farm. Run by the Twelve Tribes Community, who live communally based on the Book of Acts in the Christian bible. Not all hikers come away pleased with a visit, but you've probably read enough stories to want to see it for yourself.

- **AT Museum (Pine Grove Furnace State Park, PA).** Follow white-blazes directly to the front door of this official trail museum. View great historic displays of the Appalachian Trail and its most famous hikers. Don't forget to do your half-pint ice cream challenge next door!

- **Sunny Rest Resort (Palmerton, PA).** Clothing-optional resort with spa, campground, outdoor activities, various events and bistro.

- **Port Clinton Barber (Port Clinton, PA).** Meet Frank Russo – barber, nostalgia collector, rock musician, and friend to all thru-hikers. Stop in for haircut, or just to recharge electronics. But don't miss a chance to meet Frank over free donuts and coffee.

- **Common Ground Farm & Retreat (Three miles from Eckville, PA).** Organic farm and retreat center offering cottage stay with breakfast and shuttle to/from trail. With a mission to create a place of peace for combat veterans, Common Ground focuses on creating an environment to "disconnect with the urgent, so you can reconnect with the important." Common Ground also is notable for hosting American vets for free.

- **Deer Head Inn (Delaware Water Gap, PA).** Enjoy an evening of music at the country's oldest jazz club in continuous operation; located directly on the AT; also offers B&B rooms and meals.

- **Rickey Farm/Ministries (Vernon, NJ).** Camping permitted for thru-hikers at The Recovery Farm, a Christian ministry seeking to aid persons in recovery from addictions and personal problems.

- **Moon in the Pond Farm (Sheffield, MA).** Camping and work-for-stay at this "small, diverse, sustainable, permaculture farm" of The Berkshires. Explore the myriad of educational programs, including: animals, crops, self-sufficiency, sustainability, permaculture, ecology, conservation of heirloom vegetable varieties and seeds, conservation of historic livestock, and traditional and modern farming techniques.

- **The Cookie Lady (Becket, MA).** Serving fresh cookies to any hiker who stops by, Marilyn (and husband Roy) Wiley are trail angels that have served the AT community for over 30 years. Hikers are welcome to stop for a rest, refill water, camp in the yard, and even pick fresh blueberries from the berry farm.

- **Inn at Long Trail (Sherburne Pass, VT).** Enjoy Irish music weekends at the hiker-friendly McGrath's Pub on site, featuring authentic pours of Guinness stout.

- **Linda & Randy Hart (West Hartford, VT).** Immediately north of the White River in West Hartford, VT is the blue-painted home of Linda and Randy Hart, who open their AT-emblazoned garage loft as a bunkroom and their yard for overnight camping. The welcoming back porch always offers cold drinks and (usually) fresh baked goods, which are best enjoyed after a swim in the White River (across the street). Some braver folks may even jump in from atop the West Hartford Bridge ... though legally, we can't recommend it.

- **Mt. Cube Sugar Farm (Wentworth, NH).** Less than two miles from a trailhead, this family-owned farm that Grandma Gatewood visited still welcomes thru-hikers to camp for the night. Ask to hear the story and see photos of Grandma Gatewood.

- **White House Landing (100-Mile Wilderness, ME).** A classic off-the-grid Maine wilderness camp for all outdoor activities that welcomes thru-hikers via boat ride across Pemadumcook Lake. Lodging and meals available for a break from the 100-mile wilderness.

Best Platinum Special AT Experience:
Elmer's Sunnybank Inn (Hot Springs, NC)

In 1948 the Appalachian Trail, like today, walked straight through the town of Hot Springs, NC. This was the year that Earl Shaffer set out on his "long cruise" to become the first person ever to thru-hike the AT. When he reached Hot Springs, he spent the night at a little-known place called the Sunnybank Inn.

Today, that Inn is operated by another Elmer, Elmer Hall, who stopped at this 1840's Victorian mansion during his own thru-hike in 1976. Elmer returned in 1978 and acquired the property to run as his own.

Since that time, he has operated the Sunnybank Inn as a retreat center and hostel for AT hikers, which in 1980 was included on the National Registry of Historic Places.

Known affectionately today as just Elmer's, the Inn continues to host hundreds of thru-hikers each year. There may be no place on the Trail where such Appalachian history, culture and hospitality come together. The Inn has a feel like no other, largely due to its proprietor, who has filled the property with antiques, an extensive library, and a music room with banjo, guitar, Gentry piano, and various other instruments. Located a few steps from the AT markers set into the sidewalk concrete, there is perhaps nothing Elmer would enjoy more than for thru-hikers to slow down, rest, and visit the Inn while enjoying the vegetarian, communal meals. Not only are these organic, garden-grown meals made from scratch by Elmer, but he adds to the dining experience with a cultivation of conversation on thought-provoking topics.

Elmer is now over 80 years old, and the opportunity to share in his good graces should be had by every hiker while still available (which we hope is another 80 years). RTK stayed at Elmer's and says, "there may be no experience along the Appalachian Trail equal to that at Elmer's Sunnybank Inn."

Runners-up:
- AT Museum (Pine Grove Furnace State Park, PA)
- Kincora Hiking Hostel (Hampton, TN).
- White House Landing (100-Mile Wilderness, ME).

Honorable Mention:
- The Cookie Lady (Becket, MA)
- Linda & Randy Hart (West Hartford, VT)

Platinum Trail Towns

During a thru-hike, there will be countless stops along the way where the AT is literally white-blazed into and through certain towns. For NOBOs, Hot Springs in North Carolina is the first such town. A few hundred miles later hikers enter Virginia and walk straight through Damascus, sometimes called "Trail Town USA" for how focused the town is on hiking community.

After that comes Harper's Ferry, then Boiling Springs, Delaware Water Gap, Dalton, Cheshire, Hanover … and many more. In total, the AT walks directly through more than a dozen small towns without taking a step off the Trail. Additionally, countless towns are so close to the Trail and welcoming to hikers, that the ATC recognizes them with formal designation as AT Trail Communities. At the time of this guide's printing, there were over 40 such communities.

Listed below are the best trail towns and communities (and some of their best-of highlights) that we believe are truly platinum for stopping along a thru-hike journey.

Listing of Platinum Trail Towns

Hot Springs, NC
- Best Accommodations: Laughing Heart Lodge
- Best Hostel: Elmer's Sunnybank Inn
- Best Restaurant: Iron Horse Station
- Best Brewery/Pub: Spring Creek Tavern
- Best Special AT Experience: An evening with Elmer at Elmer's Sunnybank Inn
- Best Value Restaurant: Smokey Mountain Diner

Damascus, VA
- Best Accommodations: Old Mill Inn; Mountain Laurel Inn
- Best Hostel: Woodchuck's
- Best Restaurant: MoJo's Café

- Best Brewery/Pub: Damascus Brewery
- Best Special AT Experience: Bicycle ride along the Creeper Trail
- Best Value Restaurant: Subway

Waynesboro, VA
- Best Accommodations: The Iris Inn
- Best Restaurant: Green Leaf Grill
- Best Burger: Tailgate Grill
- Best Special AT Experience: canoe Shenandoah River
- Best Value Restaurant: Ming Garden
- Special Note: probably the best network of trail angels on the AT, be sure to get a copy of all of the locals willing to help hikers

Harper's Ferry, WV
- Best Accommodations: Lily Garden B&B; Rockhaven B&B
- Best Restaurant: The Anvil Restaurant
- Best Brewery/Pub: Potomac Grill
- Best Special AT Experience: National Historical Park; ATC Headquarters; direct train to Washington, DC

Boiling Springs, PA
- Best Accommodations: Allenberry Resort
- Best Restaurant: Boiling Springs Tavern
- Best Special AT Experience: Theater at Allenberry Resort
- Best Value Restaurant: Café 101

Delaware Water Gap, PA
- Best Accommodations: Deer Head Inn
- Best Restaurant: Sycamore Grill
- Best Special AT Experience: Live jazz music at Deer Head Inn; rafting of Delaware River
- Best Breakfast: Welsh's
- Best Value Restaurant: Village Farmer & Bakery

Pawling, NY
- Best Accommodations: Station Inn
- Best Restaurant: McKinney & Doyle

- Best Brewery/Pub: O'Conner's Public House
- Best Deli: Tony's Deli; Vinny's Deli
- Best Special AT Experience: Commuter train direct to New York City
- Best Value Restaurant: Gaudino's Pizza & Pasta

Manchester Center, VT
- Best Accommodations: Reluctant Panther Inn
- Best Hostel: Green Mountain Hostel
- Best Restaurant: Mulligan's Pub & Restaurant; Silver Fork
- Best Breakfast: Up for Breakfast
- Best Deli: Zoey's
- Best Burger: Zoey's
- Best Special AT Experience: American Museum of Fly Fishing, Manchester Riverwalk
- Best Value Restaurant: Cilantro Taco

Hanover, NH
- Best Accommodations: Hanover Inn
- Best Restaurant: Molly's Restaurant
- Best Brewery/Pub: Murphy's on the Green
- Best Special AT Experience: Dartmouth College museums and performing arts centers
- Special Note: a wonderful network of Trail Angels offering to shuttle or house hikers in an otherwise expensive town

Gorham, NH
- Best Accommodations: The Libby House Inn
- Best Hostel: Rattle River Lodge & Hostel (technically in Shelburne)
- Best Restaurant: Libby's Bistro & SAalt Pub
- Best Breakfast: Welsh's Restaurant
- Best Special AT Experience: Mt. Washington Cog Railway; Wildcat Mountain gondola
- Best Value Restaurant: Mr. Pizza

Rangeley, ME
- Best Accommodations: Rangeley Inn
- Best Hostel: The Hiker Hut
- Best Restaurant: Hungry Trout
- Best Brewery/Pub: Sarge's Sports Pub & Grub
- Best Burger: Sarge's Sports Pub & Grub
- Best Special AT Experience: Swimming, boating, fishing, or cruise on Rangeley Lake
- Best Value Restaurant: The Shed BBQ

Caratunk, ME
- Best Accommodations: Sterling Inn; Northern Outdoors
- Best Hostel: Caratunk House
- Best Brewery/Pub: Kennebec River Brewery
- Best Special AT Experience: rafting on the Kennebec River
- Best Value Restaurant: Northern Outdoors

Monson, ME
- Best Accommodations: Lakeshore House Lodge
- Best Hostel: Shaw's Hiker Hostel
- Best Restaurant: Lakeshore House Restaurant
- Best Breakfast: Shaw's Hiker Hostel
- Best Special AT Experience: Monson AT Visitor Center
- Best Value Restaurant: Spring Creek BBQ

Best Platinum Trail Town:

Hot Springs, NC

That first time an AT thru-hiker walks along the white-blazed Main Street of a small town is a special moment. And Hot Springs, with AT symbols engraved into the town's sidewalks and telephone poles, is the best for not just being first but also best well-rounded. A non-hiker may not give Hot Springs a second glance, but it is easy to understand why most hikers consider this to be the best town along the entire Trail. Hot Springs has history, the French Broad River, natural mineral springs (hot tubs), a large and thru-hiker focused outfitter, a welcoming and helpful community, numerous lodging options, a number of good and hiker friendly restaurants, and AT legend Elmer Hall at the Sunnybank Inn.

For NOBOs, Hot Springs also provides the first real stop after completing the Great Smoky Mountains, a pivotal achievement thus far on the thru-hike. It is common for thru-hikers to take at least one zero day when they reach Hot Springs, and we think it is easily worth the long stop.

Runners-Up:
- Manchester Center, VT
- Gorham, NH

Up and Coming:
- Pawling, NY

Platinum City Visits & Unique Side Trips

As an AT thru-hiker winds their way from Georgia to Maine, numerous opportunities exist to get off the Trail completely and experience the best cities and sites in this part of America. Destinations like downtown Atlanta or New York City are literally visible from high points on the Trail, and other well-known historic sites, such as the American Civil War battlefield and museum at Gettysburg, are less than an hour drive away.

Although exciting and different, these big cities and unique side trips in a thru-hike require significant travel and time off the Trail, so it is unlikely every thru-hiker will take them all in. However, sometimes getting significantly off the Trail to visit America's iconic destinations is exactly what you need to continue the path onward. In fact, a good Platinum-Blazer will have some of these stops in mind from the outset, as there is no better way to luxury thru-hike ... than to not be a thru-hiker at all for a few days.

Although you can always have a friend, shuttle or car service pick you up at any nearby trailhead, we included the best access point using public transportation or direct routes below to help make visiting these locations as logistically simple as possible.

Listing of Platinum City Visits & Unique Side Trips:

Atlanta, GA
- Reasons to Visit: Major US city and capitol of Georgia; major southeast city with gardens, art museums, fine dining; major league sports teams; civil war & civil rights history.
- Best Access: Before starting a NOBO thru-hike, also by car from Amicalola Falls State Park or Mountain Crossings (Blairsville, GA).

Dahlonega, GA
- Reasons to Visit: Gold rush history; access northern GA wine country; outdoor activities.

- Best Access: Before starting a NOBO thru-hike, also by car from Amicalola Falls State Park or Mountain Crossings (Blairsville, GA).

Helen, GA

- Reasons to Visit: Bavarian-themed town; access to North Georgia Wine country.
- Best Access: Car/shuttle from Unicoi Gap (GA) or Mountain Crossings (GA).

Gatlinburg, TN

- Reasons to Visit: Family oriented vacation resort town; Great Smoky Mountains, moonshine distilleries.
- Best Access: Car/shuttle from Newfound Gap (GSMNP).

Ashville, NC

- Reasons to Visit: Cultural center for many outdoor activities, arts, music & craft breweries; access to Mt. Mitchell (highest peak east of Mississippi); Grove Park Inn; Biltmore Mansion & Winery.
- Best Access: Car from Hot Springs (NC).

Johnson City, TN

- Reasons to Visit: Biking, caving, climbing and other outdoor sports; frontier history.
- Best Access: Car from Roan Mountain (TN) or Lake Watauga (TN).

Damascus, VA

- Reasons to Visit: Creeper Bike Trail. Trail Days hiker festival.
- Best Access: Directly on the AT.

Blacksburg, VA

- Reasons to Visit: Virginia Tech college town, New River Gorge, outdoor activities.
- Best Access: Car from Atkins (VA), Catawba (VA), Pearisburg (VA).

Roanoke, VA

- Reasons to visit: Hotel Roanoke; canoeing, mountain biking, horseback riding.
- Best Access: Car from Catawba (VA), Daleville (VA), or Troutville (VA).

Charlottesville, VA

- Reasons to Visit: University of Virginia college town; wine region; Monticello (Thomas Jefferson's home).
- Best Access: Bus/car from Waynesboro (VA); Swift Run Gap (SNP).

Waynesboro, VA

- Reasons to Visit: Access to Shenandoah National Park and the Shenandoah River; canoeing, rafting, kayaking and other outdoor sports.
- Best Access: Car/shuttle from US 250 trailhead at Rockfish Gap/Afton Mountain.

Washington, VA

- Reasons to Visit: The Inn at Little Washington has been listed as one of the Top 10 restaurants in the world; Recognized as the first establishment to ever receive five stars for both its accommodations and cuisine – now that's platinum, a distinction The Inn still maintains.
- Best Access: Thornton Gap (Shenandoah National Park); Front Royal (VA).

Harper's Ferry, WV

- Reasons to Visit: American colonial and civil war history; Canoeing, rafting, or kayaking on Potomac and Shenandoah rivers.
- Best Access: Directly on AT.

Washington, DC

- Reasons to Visit: Our nation's capital; political, historical, and cultural center.
- Best Access: Bus/car from Waynesboro (VA), car from Thornton Gap (SNP), or train from Harpers Ferry (WV).

Sharpsburg/Antietam, MD

- Reasons to Visit: American Civil War battlefield.
- Best Access: Car from Harpers Ferry (WV) or car/walk from Boonsboro, (MD).

Gettysburg, PA

- Reasons to Visit: American civil war battlefield and museum.
- Best Access: Car from US 30 Highway at mile 1083.6 (PA); Waynesboro (PA), Fayetteville (PA), Boiling Springs (PA).

Harrisburg, PA

- Reasons to Visit: Capitol of Pennsylvania; Canoeing, rafting, kayak on the Susquehanna River; Hersheypark amusement park; Carlisle auto shows.
- Best Access: Car from Boiling Springs (PA) or Duncannon (PA).

Pottsville, PA

- Reasons to Visit: D.G. Yuengling and Sons Brewery (oldest brewery in America).
- Best Access: Car from Port Clinton (PA).

Delaware Water Gap, PA

- Reasons to Visit: Canoeing, rafting, kayaking; COTA jazz festival.
- Best Access: Directly on the AT.

West Point, NY

- Reasons to Visit: Strategic fortification on the Hudson River during the American Revolution and home of the United States Military Academy since 1802.
- Best Access: Car from Bear Mountain/Fort Montgomery (NY).

New York City, NY

- Reasons to Visit: It's NYC.
- Best Access: Bus/car from Delaware Water Gap (PA) or Fort Montgomery (NY), or train from Pawling (NY).

Albany, NY

- Reasons to Visit: State capitol of New York; Shaker Heritage Society; access to the Erie Canal.
- Best Access: Bus/car from Sheffield (MA), Great Barrington (MA), or Bennington (VT).

Lenox, MA

- Reasons to Visit: Tanglewood performing arts center and the ultimate Platinum-Blazing event: annual 4th of July fireworks and concert with James Taylor; access to The Berkshires
- Best Access: Car from Lee (MA) or Dalton (MA).

Boston, MA

- Reasons to Visit: Major US city and capital of Massachusetts; American colonial/revolutionary history; major league sports teams, access to Atlantic Ocean.
- Best Access: Bus/car from North Adams (MA) or Hanover (NH).

Williamstown, MA

- Reasons to Visit: Williams College town; golf courses, art museums.
  Best Access: Car/walk from MA 2 trail crossing in North Adams (MA).

Hanover, NH

- Reasons to Visit: Dartmouth College town; Hood Museum of Art; theater and other live entertainment at Hopkins Center.
- Best Access: Directly on the AT.

North Woodstock/Lincoln, NH

- Reasons to Visit: Mountain biking, climbing, kayaking and other outdoor sports.
- Best Access: Car/shuttle from Kinsman Notch (NH) or Franconia Notch (NH).

Caratunk, ME

- Reasons to Visit: Kennebec River and Penobscot River canoeing & rafting.
- Best Access: Directly on the AT.

Bar Harbor, ME
- Reasons to Visit: Acadia National Park; lobster; maritime recreational activities; seals, puffins & whales; rocky coast & lighthouses.
- Best Access: Bus/car from Millinocket (ME).

Portland, ME
- Reasons to Visit: Largest city in Maine; lobsters & seafood cuisine; maritime activities, history & lighthouses.
- Best Access: Bus/car from Millinocket, ME.

Quebec City, Canada
- Reasons to Visit: French colonial history; Old Quebec (World Heritage Site); Montmorency Falls; Chateau Frontenac Hotel; French Canadian culture.
- Best Access: Bus/car from Millinocket, ME.

To best experience these side trips, you will simply need to arrange a shuttle, taxi or Uber/Lyft. Some have direct access via public transportation, but routes and schedules may only run on specific days or times (e.g. the Appalachian Trail train station only runs on weekends), so check schedules closely while planning.

Best Platinum City Visit:
New York City

As we said above, "it's New York City," need anyone say anything more?

AT Museum (Pine Grove Furnace State Park)

Chapter 10

THE PLATINUM CIRCLE

The Platinum Circle looks back on and summarizes below the Platinum Award winners for each category in this guide. To earn the right to call yourself a Platinum-Blazer, a good number of these locations should be part of your thru-hike experience.

In addition, we include a special "shout out" here to the AMC Hut system in the White Mountains. Because of the incredible platinum experience they offer to thru-hikers and others alike, we have dedicated a special Award of Merit to the AMC. Although rare to visit them all, a thru-hiker should consider themselves fortunate to stay in at least one of the AMC huts before reaching Gorham, NH and exiting the Whites.

Authors' Special Award of Merit

Overnight at the AMC Huts (White Mountains, NH). In the White Mountains of New Hampshire, the Appalachian Mountain Club (AMC) runs a series of huts along this section of the AT. Subject to availability (during high seasons reservations are highly recommended), thru-hikers can reserve an evening at a hut, which includes a bunk, dinner, and breakfast for approximately $100/night. Alternatively, thru-hikers can "work-for-stay", which provides a spot to sleep on the floor inside, and meal leftovers in exchange for cleaning and other odd jobs. Both Sharkbait and RTK enjoyed these huts in the standard and work-for-stay style and recommend the former for the true platinum experience.

Pure Platinum Award

Woods Hole Hostel (Giles County, VA). We introduced Woods Hole at the start of this guide because of the truly special experience it offers thru-hikers. As indicated above, we consider Woods Hole Hostel the single best overall experience along the Appalachian Trail.

Best Platinum Hotel, Resort or Lodge

Allenberry Resort (Boiling Springs, PA). A short, but uphill walk east off the Trail and just out of "downtown" Boiling Springs, PA is the Allenberry Resort. With a recent ownership change, the rooms and common areas have all be refreshed and renovated. Not only are the rooms impeccable but the related amenities are exceptional . . . which even include the Allenberry Playhouse, where thru-hikers can enjoy live theater.

Best Platinum Bed & Breakfast

Mountain Harbour B &B. Perhaps better known as a good hostel and for its extraordinary breakfast, our selection of Mountain Harbour as the Best Platinum Bed & Breakfast is to remind Platinum-Blazers that exceptional, private guest rooms are also waiting for them at this well-known stop just off the AT in the Roan Highlands.

Best Platinum Hostel

Green Mountain Hostel (Manchester Center, VT). A very well-traveled hiker on the AT told RTK that he had to stop at Green Mountain Hostel. He did and he was not disappointed, in fact, RTK was amazed at the standards of quality, cleanliness, friendliness and services at this hostel located in the middle of your journey through Vermont. Not surprisingly then that many others thought the same thing, which made Green Mountain Hostel our selection in Best Hostels as the very Best Platinum Hostel along the Appalachian Trail.

Best Platinum Restaurant

Dinner at Caffé Rel (Franklin, NC). The gas station ambiance does nothing to prevent the extraordinary, largely French, cuisine from making Caffé Rel our surprise selection as the very Best Platinum Restaurant experience along the Appalachian Trail.

Best Platinum Breakfast

Breakfast at Quarter Way Inn hostel (Ceres, VA). In April of 2018 thru-hikers had to think twice about a 0.8 mile road walk to this hostel. By June the side trip was only 0.3 miles because of a Trail rerouting. We have to say that even if the diversion was still almost a mile, the visit to Quarter Way Inn is well worth it, especially for Tina's extraordinary breakfast, which we identify above as the very Best Platinum Breakfast along the AT.

Best Platinum Ice Cream/Milkshakes

Ice Cream at Bellvale Farms Creamery (Bellvale, NY). Welcome to New York! We cannot think of a better way to relax after the challenging, yet enjoyable Prospect Rock then a stop at Bellvale Creamery, the very Best Platinum Ice Cream/Milkshake on the Appalachian Trail. A simple 0.3 walk west includes a stop at the Hot Dogs Plus stand before reaching the top of a ridge below Mount Peter, where the only thing more spectacular than the view back to High Point Monument is the ice cream, shakes and sundaes.

Best Platinum Brewery and Pub

Devil's Backbone (Roseland, VA). The winner of our Best Platinum Brewery and Pub, the reasons to stop here continue to multiply. For 2019, Devils' Backbone has formalized a shuttle service to/from the Trail to make an overnight stay and its hiker breakfast more readily available.

Best Platinum Deli

Horler's Store (Unionville, N Y). Deli-Blazing really only begins in New Jersey for northbound thru-hikers. After a few practice days, be sure to take the 0.5-mile diversion and stop at Horler's Store for what we think is the Best Platinum Deli along the Trail.

Best Platinum Burger

The Doyle (Duncannon, PA). There's no shortage of opinions about the famous or infamous Doyle Hotel. Our thoughts are fairly simple, we think everyone should at least stop to enjoy the Best Platinum Burger along the AT (the variety of Yuengling on tap is not too bad either).

Best Platinum Pizza

Anile's Ristorante & Pizzeria (Boiling Springs, PA). Anile's almost made the best restaurant category, but truthfully the only thing to get here is pizza. This family-owned restaurant is just a couple hundred feet down the road from the Appalachian Trail Conservancy office in Boiling Springs, and provides the Best Platinum Pizza to be had on the AT.

Best Platinum Value Restaurant

The Homeplace (Catawba, VA). If there is one award that we might never hear debate about, it would be selecting The Homeplace as the Best Platinum Value Restaurant with its welcoming atmosphere and service and its exceptional, all-you-can-eat dinner of classic, southern cooking. It has long been very popular with thru-hikers as they come off Dragon's Tooth outside of Roanoke, Virginia.

Best Platinum Blue-Blaze Hike

Gulf Hagas (100-Mile Wilderness, ME). If we had to select the single Best Platinum Blue-Blaze Hike, we'd have to make it long enough and memorable enough to stand out among the 2,200 other miles hiked.

The Gulf Hagas gorge fits the bill. It has to be special, unique and epic to be the "Grand Canyon of the East." We think you'll find it worthwhile and look back on slowing down for half of a day in the 100-Mile Wilderness as a very good decision.

Best Platinum Special AT Experience

Elmer and his Sunnybank Inn (Hot Springs, NC). This Trail legend's own brand of hospitality, including special, communal meals makes this our Best Platinum Special AT Experience.

Best Platinum Trail Town

Hot. Springs, NC. A collection of great experiences, an excellent outfitter, and standout meal opportunities make the very walkable and comfortable Hot Springs our Best Platinum Trail Town.

Best Platinum City Visit

New York City. Few destinations rate above New York as the city more individuals worldwide want to visit. Why would thru-hikers be any different?

AMC's Galehead Hut (White Mountains

APPENDIX

"YaYa" - Hot Springs, NC shuttle driver

Other Notable Favorites, Winners, and Mentions

In addition to our listings of platinum experiences and our category winners, we'd like to give a quick shout out to these other people and places worthy of note along the AT in some miscellaneous categories. Although they did not make the cut for a listing or chapter of their own, these were some of our favorite experiences along the Trail that we felt needed special consideration for any future hiker.

Best Unique Dinner experience:
Elmer's Sunnybank Inn (Hot Springs, NC)
Woods Hole Hostel (Giles County, VA)

Best Private Accommodations at a Hostel:
The Franklin Room at Rattle River Lodge & Hostel (Shelburne, NH)

Best Shuttle Driver:
George Lightcap (central NJ);
Mike Gelinas (central PA)
Bubba Barnes (Southern/Western VA)
Adam ("Stanimal") Stanley (central VA)

Best Hostel Host:
Paul Fuller (Caratunk House)
Paul Stream (Libby Barn)
Lois ("Mosey") Kowalyk (Mosey's Place)

Best Atmosphere/Vibe:
Caratunk House
Libby Barn

Most Underrated Stop:
Cumberland Farms (especially in Dalton, MA & Gorham, ME)

Biggest Disappointments & Most Squandered Opportunities:

Here at the Platinum-Blaze we want to celebrate the best, but we also want to alert hikers to places that disappointed. Some of the more noteworthy memories are below, which we believe missed an opportunity to offer excellent experiences to thru-hikers. We highlight a few below, and hope they improve their thru-hiker status in future years to make this guide's platinum listings.

- **Walasi-Yi hostel (Mountain Crossings, GA).** Could there be a better location or time for a thru-hiker to be welcomed by a great hostel stay than here at Mountain Crossings – all NOBO thru-hikers first real stop after the first few days of an end-to-end hike? Could you be any more disappointed than considering a stay at the hostel there? Fortunately, a northbound thru-hiker has a better alternative just a few hundred yards away at the Blood Mountain Cabins, which includes laundry and a general store with reasonably good pizza and other choices on-site. All that said, Mountain Crossings is an excellent (albeit overpriced) outfitter, and a worthwhile stop early in one's hike.

- **The Summit B&B (Port Andreas, PA).** Formerly the Blue Mountain Summit B&B, we hope the new management will get things figured out for future hikers (including remembering reservations). Good bar. Good food. Barely average, private rooms at platinum prices, and a sad, DIY continental breakfast. The Summit does, however, appear to have a welcoming spirit for hikers including an attractive, outdoor space, and excellent tenting ground. Less than 0.1M off the Trail, The Summit should use its proximity to work itself into these platinum listings.

- **Anton's on the Lake (Greenwood Lake, NY).** Although it has a reputation for a relaxing, platinum stay, RTK's numerous calls and emails were never returned.

- **Bascom Lodge - Mt. Greylock (MA).** There may be no spot directly on the Trail with such an opportunity to offer an exciting, platinum stay. Sitting on the summit of Mt. Greylock, this lodge offers private rooms, a bunkbed, hostel room, meals, and best of all, a chance to enjoy sunsets, stars and sunrises. Sadly, though, the hostel is average, the motel-like, private rooms with shared, hall bathroom are overpriced, and the staff barely acknowledges the hiker community. Someone should speak with the AMC-Berkshire Chapter and the Commonwealth of Massachusetts.

Mt. Greylock (Massachusetts)

The New England B&B Challenge

While traversing through CT, MA and VT, a savvy hiker can stay every night in a first-class, Bed & Breakfast or Inn. This trek can be completed in approximately three weeks and represents the truest form of Platinum-Blazing any hiker can do in New England. In fact, if any readers of this guide complete the suggested recommended itinerary below, they can reach out to us at admin@platinum-blazing.com for a special Platinum-Blaze Certificate of Distinction.

Day	Mile	Trailhead	Town Stop
0	1450	NY 22	Station Inn – 2.6E (Pawling, NY)
Connecticut			
Start this "Bed & Breakfast Blazing" by leaving the NY 22 trailhead at the AT railroad stop outside Pawling, NY and then entering New England later that day.			
1	1468	CT 341	Fife 'n Drum Inn – 1.1E (Kent, CT)
2	1480	CT 4	Cornwall Inn – 3.2E (Cornwall Bridge, CT)
3	1493	Water Street	Falls Village Inn – 0.2E (Falls Village, CT)
4	1500	U.S. 44	White Hart Inn – 0.6W (Salisbury, CT)
Massachusetts			
The AT through CT seems made for B&B-blazing. With nice spacing of idyllic town stops with great inns and fine restaurants, a platinum-blazer will have trouble passing up this four-day luxury walk, which ends perfectly with a nero in Salisbury.			
5	1518	Side Trail off AT	Egremont Village Inn – 1.2W (Egremont, MA)
5/6	1522	U.S. 7	Many options – 3.0W (Great Barrington, MA)
6/7	1541	Jerusalem Rd	Devonfield Inn – 6.8W (Tyringham, MA)
8	1550	U.S. 20	Devonfield Inn. - 6.2W (Lee, MA)
8	1560	Washington Mtn Rd	Maplewood B&B – 6.3E (Dalton, MA)
9	1570	MA 8 & 9	Harbour House Inn – 11.0E (Cheshire, MA)
10	1579	Main Street	Harbour House Inn – 1.0E (Cheshire, MA)
10/11	1587	Mt. Greylock	Bascom Lodge (on the AT)
11/12	1593	MA 2	Williams Inn – 3.0W (Williamstown, MA)

		Vermont	
B&B-blazing through MA has more options but requires. more shuttles (check with each B&B) and requires a few long (18-20 miles) days, but if combined with slackpacking and/or a zero day in Williamstown) it too can be a fairly luxurious experience. With so many options so close together, this state could be done in a few days.			
13	1612	VT 9	Four Chimneys Inn – 5.2W (Bennington, VT)
14	1632	USFS 71 (gravel)	Inn at Mt. Snow – 14.0E (West Dover, VT)
15	1638	Stratton Mtn Tower	Stratton Mtn Resort – 0.8E (take gondola down)
16	1652	VT 11 & 30	Reluctant Panther Inn – 5.0W (Manchester, VT)
17	1670	Danby-Landgrove Rd	IB Munson House – 12.0W (Wallingford, VT)
18	1678	VT 140	Clifford Country B&B – 6.1E (Mount Holly, VT)
19	1695	Killington Resort	Killington Resort – 0.2E (Killington, VT)
20	1706	Kent Pond	Mountain Meadows Lodge (on AT)
21	1725	VT 12	Village Inn of Woodstock – 4.1E (Woodstock, VT)
22	1739	VT 14	Quechee Inn – 6.6E (Quechee, VT)
23	1747	VT 5 (Main St)	Norwich Inn – 0.1W (Norwich, VT)
Vermont also offers some beautiful towns that more typically welcome skiers and leaf-peepers. To fully B&B-blaze Vermont, the hiker will need to fit in a few 20-mile days, but there are also options for a zero day or a couple of nero days to help soak in the experience. At least with great trails and nimble shuttles (and perhaps some slackpacking), this state too can be blazed luxuriously.			
23	1749	NH 10A	Hanover Inn – 0.0W (Hanover, NH)
B&Bs in NH are less prominent and more difficult to access due to the distances between and from trailheads. However, one can complete the New England B&B Challenge by crossing the Connecticut River into Hanover, NH and staying at the Hanover Inn (whose accommodations are finer than Norwich, VT on the other side of the river).			

Platinum-Blazing's
Deli-Blazing Itinerary

Deli-Blazing Itinerary

Use this suggested itinerary for "deli-blazing" along the AT from New Jersey to Vermont. Although the frequency of stops dissipates by the time you reach the Green Mountain State, these lunch stops will make for great lunch breaks along this 500+ mile stretch.

New Jersey				
Day	*Mile*	*Trailhead*	*MOT**	*Name of Deli*
			(*Miles Off Trail)	
1	1305	Camp Road (gravel)	0.3W	"deli" counter in AMC Mohican Center
2	1323	Culvers Gap-US 206		
			0.2W	Gyp's Tavern
			0.8	Culver Lake Farm Market
			1.6E	Dale's Deli (Branchville)
			2.5E	Yellow Cottage Deli/Bakery (Branchville)
3	1337	NJ 23		
			0.7W	seasonal concession at Lake Marcia
			4.4W	Woogie's Deli (Port Jervis)
4	1346	Lott Road	0.7	Horler's Store (Unionville, NY)
4	1354	County 515	1.1W	Pochuck Valley Farm Market & Deli

5	1358	NJ 94		
			0.1W	Heaven Hill Farm
			0.1W	Mitch's Hot Dog stand
			2.4E	ACME Market (Vernon, NJ)
			2.4E	Healthy Thymes Market (Vernon, NJ)

New York

6	1373	NY 17A		
			0.1W	Hot dogs plus
			0.2W	Bellvale Farms Creamery
			1.6W	Bellvale Deli
			2.0E	Greenwood Lake (restaurants) access by GL Vista Trail off AT (0.9)
7	1390	Tiorati Circle	0.3E	Uber to Bear Mountain/Ft. Montgomery
8	1404	Bear Mountain Inn		
			0.1E	Hiker's Café (inside Bear Mountain Inn)
			0	concessions (seasonal)
			0.9W	Fort Montgomery (Country Deli)
9	1411	U.S. 9	0	Appalachian Market/Café/Deli
10	1423	NY 301	1.0E	Clarence Fahnestock State Park
11	1435	NY 52	0.3E	Mountain Top deli
11	1442	NY 55	1.5W	A & A Deli
11/ 12	1447	West Dover Rd	3.2E	Vinny's Deli (Pawling, NY)
12	1450	NY 22 (AT RR Stop)		
			0	food truck
			0.7E	Tony's Deli
			2.6W	Ben's Deli

12	1453	Pawling Nature Trail	0.9W	Ben's Deli

<table>
<tr><td colspan="5" align="center">Connecticut</td></tr>
</table>

13	1461	Bull's Bridge Road	0.5E	Bull's Bridge Country Market
13	1468	CT 341	0.7E	Kent Market/deli (Kent)
14	1480	CT 4	0.9E	Cornwall Country Market/deli
15	1493	Water Street	0.3E	Toymaker's Café (Falls Village)
15/16	1500	U.S. 44	0.4W	LaBonne's Market (Salisbury) W at Cobble Rd
15/16	1501	Undermountain Rd	0.8W	LaBonne's Market (Salisbury) W

<table>
<tr><td colspan="5" align="center">Massachusetts</td></tr>
</table>

17	1518	MA 41		
			1.2W	Egremont Market
			1.2W	Mom's Country Cafe
17	1522	U.S. 7		
			1.6W	Guido's Fresh Marketplace/deli
			1.8W	Great Barrington, MA
			3.2E	Marketplace Kitchen/Café (Sheffield, MA)
18	1541	Jerusalem Road or Main Street	5.0W	Big Y Deli. (Lee, MA)
19	1550	U.S. 20		Lee, MA
20	1560	Washington Mtn Rd	10W	Dalton, MA
20	1570	MA 8 & 9		
				Angelina's Subs (Dalton, MA)
				Jacob's Pub (Dalton, MA)
				Dalton General Store (Dalton, MA)

21	1579	Main Street		Diane's Twist (Cheshire, MA)
22	1587	Mt. Greylock		Bascom Lodge
23	1593	MA 2		Wild Oaks (deli) (Williamstown)

Vermont

24	1612	VT 9		Henry's Market (Bennington)
27	1652	VT 11	2.4E	Bromley Market
			5.4E	Zoey's Deli (Manchester Center)
28	1670	Danby-Landgrove Rd	3.5W	Nichols Store &Deli
29	1684	VT 103	0.8W	Loretta's Good Food Deli
30	1702	U.S. 4		
			0.9E	Inn at Long Trail (McGrath's Pub)
			8.6W	Yellow Deli (Rutland)
			1.8E	Killington Deli & Marketplace (Killington)
32	1725	VT 12		
			0.2W	On the Edge Farm
			4.2E	Village Butcher Shop (Woodstock, VT)
34	1747	VT 5	0.1W	Dan & Whit's (Norwich, VT)

New Hampshire

34	1749 .5	NH 120	0.05W	Co-Op Food Stores (Hanover, NH

Acknowledgements

First and foremost, the authors want to thank their wives, Cheryl and Dana, for the wonderful support throughout their thru-hikes. They put up with quite a bit in letting us pursue this adventure ... and the continued obsession afterwards for all things Appalachian Trail.

RTK is indebted to Stacy Beaulieu for so enthusiastically serving as his personal concierge for the entire journey, to Ryan Kelly for editing and uploading his weekly blogs, and to Stacy again for compiling, editing and uploading his YouTube videos. He is particularly grateful to the numerous friends that followed along, and particularly to, Brooke, Randy, Mike, Ned & Kathy, Mike & Pam, Wally, Rob, Barb, Amy, and Jim, all of whom came out and hiked with him for a day or several days.

Sharkbait could never thank all the family and friends that helped make this dream a reality, but special shout out goes to Craig, Rob, Mikey, Max, Aaron, and Adam for making their way to the trail to be part of it with him. Additionally, no amount of thanks could match the love and support received from Tom (Happy), Kevin, Devorah, Jonah, Caleb, and Zachary from start to finish. Every moment they joined him on the trail was platinum in and of itself.

Lastly, we are grateful to our many 2018 fellow thru-hikers for participating in the survey that helped to validate the listings and selections in this guide. Finally, a special thanks to Dan "Scars" Harris, Allen "Atlas" Thomas, and Paul "Seven" Castillo for their valuable comments about and edits to the manuscript for this book.

- Sharkbait & RTK

About the Authors

Bruce "RTK" Matson & Michael "Sharkbait" Neiman both completed northbound thru-hikes of the Appalachian Trail in 2018. A lawyer from Richmond, Virginia for over 35 years, RTK now helps to lead a patent analytics and litigation finance company. Sharkbait traveled from sunny Los Angeles to hike the Trail, and loved it so much he moved to Northern Virginia afterwards. He is a human resources technology consultant in the hospitality industry in the Washington DC metro area.

RTK and Sharkbait met online while individually preparing for their hikes, and although started a few weeks apart, met up in Virginia in person – but only twice; once near Chestnut Knob in a freezing fog and then during a beautiful, sunny zero day at Woods Hole. Through their personal blogs and podcasts, they kept up on each other's whereabouts throughout the trail, and remain close friends and hiking partners today.

****

Please reach out to the authors at admin@platinum-blazing.com if you have comments, suggestions or would like to be considered for the editorial board (The Platinum Blaze Institute) for the future (annual) editions of *Platinum-Blazing the Appalachian Trail: How to Thru-hike in 5 3-Star Luxury*.

Additional copies of this guide are available from (i) Amazon, (ii) www.platinum-blazing.com, or (iii) the authors, who are happy to personalize copies as requested.

Made in the USA
Middletown, DE
29 July 2023

35871621R00086